PRAISE FOR

BECOME LIKE CAPTAIN MORONI

"I love this book! As a parent of a teenager and with two more on the rise (yikes), I am constantly searching for ways to fortify their budding testimonies, defend them from temptation, help them become strong in the gospel, and help them to become genuinely good human beings. This book has added another arrow to not only my quiver but to my childrens' as well. Sean Nobmann reintroduces well-known characters in a way that makes them funny, approachable, and real. We see them teach and liken the scriptures to themselves throughout the book, meaningfully expanding the scriptures without the reader even realizing it. I found myself entertained and buoyed up! It was full of new insights into well-known stories as well as memorable moments and phrases that will offer support and strength long after the book has been put down. Thank you for writing this!"

—BRIAN NEAL CLARK, father, husband, film and stage actor, singer, and interior designer

"I wish this book had been available when I was a young man; it makes the scriptures even cooler than they already are. Reading Sean Nobmann's unique and engaging writing style today, I found myself learning things from the scriptures I never knew were there, and laughing all along the way. I was spiritually edified by this incredible read and grateful for the actionable takeaways designed to help me protect myself and my family from negative influences. Every youth and every parent in every religion will benefit from reading this book. Sean Nobmann has created his own genre, a powerfully lighthearted take on the sacred and special. Not only will youth learn and be uplifted by this awesome read, this book will change the lives of any who pick it up."

—JASON HEWLETT, CSP, CPAE, husband, father, Speaker Hall of Fame inductee, author, musician, award-winning entertainer

BECOME LIKE CAPTAIN MORONI

SEAN NOBMANN
NORMAN SHURTLIFF

ISBN 13: 978-1-4621-4606-2

Published by CFI, an imprint of Cedar Fort, Inc.
2373 W. 700 S., Suite 100 Springville, UT 84663
Distributed by Cedar Fort, Inc., www.cedarfort.com

Library of Congress Registration Number: 2018036888

Cover design by Norman Shurtliff and Shawnda T. Craig

Edited and typeset by Nicole Terry

Printed in the United States of America

10 9 8 7 6 5 4 3 2 1

Printed on acid-free paper

For Katherine, Harrison, Asher,
Lincoln, and Jonathan

ALSO BY

SEAN NOBMANN

A Mid-Life American Dream: The Rise of Angel Groups

ALSO BY

NORMAN SHURTLIFF

Amazing Scriptures: A Book of Mormon Adventure of Comics and Mazes!

Skull Cat: Skull Cat and the Curious Castle

CONTENTS

ACKNOWLEDGMENTS

In the winter of 2003, my wonderful elders quorum president, Darron Ohlwiler, asked me to teach a lesson on overcoming temptation to the elders in our young married student ward. After several days of study and prayer, I had the thought, *Wow, it's almost like Amalickiah IS temptation.* Immediately, I felt the Spirit confirm the idea. I paced my small apartment in wonder as I continued to feel a powerful, confirming spirit for several minutes. I immediately went back and reread all of the Captain Moroni and Amalickiah chapters before creating a lesson that wasn't mine but rather felt like it had been pushed off of a heavenly shelf and into my lap. I taught the lesson in that ward and have taught it in several wards since. In 2016, Jason Casperson heard me teach it to a group of deacons and asked me to write it down for him. Without Jason's encouragement, I don't believe this book would have happened.

I am so thankful for Jessica Pettit for believing in me. She has been a great blessing and resource throughout this process, as has everyone at Cedar Fort. Bryce Mortimer, Nicole Terry, Kaitlin Barwick, Kathryn Watkins, and Vikki Downs have helped so much along the way. I am also forever grateful to Cheri Christensen for her editing expertise, which cleaned up a lot of errors and drivel from my first draft. Others who provided invaluable edits include Marshall Lamm, Brandilyn Haynes, Jocelyn and Paul Pedersen, and Brent Barney. Jacob Prestwich, a college roommate of mine and a great friend, really went above and beyond. He even enlisted two priests from his ward, Carter Martin and Ethan Baum, to review the manuscript and provide feedback and edits from their perspectives. Carter and Ethan: thank you for your help! You really added a lot to the final product! Thank you all for being willing to nourish, dig about, and prune my writing. It needed it!

I am so grateful for my illustrator, Norman Shurtliff. He brought his own vision, hard work, and talent to the story. His artwork adds so much to the final result. I am lucky to have him. Finally, I owe so much to my wife, Katherine, and our four sons: Harrison, Asher, Lincoln, and Jonathan. I hope this book projects half as much goodness as Katherine does on a daily basis. Her fingerprints are all over every page. Her suggestions were valuable, insightful, and immeasurable.

Smart, funny, and talented people may recommend this book on the back cover, but even more important to me is the fact that my sons like this book. I know from experience that they don't sugarcoat their feedback, so I feel pretty confident saying that if they like it, you will too.

A NOTE TO THE READER

This book imagines that Captain Moroni and his friends are visiting from heaven, finally fulfilling a wish to personally share their story with you. Theirs is a true story taken from the scriptures, but told from a modern perspective and in their "own" words. They fill in a lot of gaps that aren't necessarily addressed in the Book of Mormon. Therefore, this book is more like a work of realistic or historical fiction than purely nonfiction. Some stories and characters have been combined, and creative license has been taken, much as is done in movies about real events, even in movies produced by The Church of Jesus Christ of Latter-day Saints. That being said, none of these changes disrupt the doctrine or the spirit of the events that actually occurred. I invite you to compare the story here with the story in your scriptures, to find these small changes for yourself, and then to linger in the scriptures for a while longer . . .

Yea, verily, verily I say unto you, if all men had been,
and were, and ever would be, like unto Moroni,
behold, the very powers of hell would have been
shaken forever; yea, the devil would never have
power over the hearts of the children of men.

ALMA 48:17

-NS

CHAPTER 1

INTRODUCTION

MORONI: While you're reading this book, every now and then let out a little sigh of exasperation, like this is the lamest book you've ever read in your entire life. Then, look up and politely ask, "Hey, Mom, do you think maybe you could make me a glass of chocolate milk to drink while I read this Captain Moroni book?" Trust me, as long as you're reading this book, you're golden! The chocolate milk will flow like the fountains on Temple Square.

For some reason, I have a magical effect on parents' brains. Parents *love* me. You should have seen when I was dating my future wife and she brought me home to meet her parents for the first time. Her dad wanted to "hang out" with me the whole time. He kept trying to show off his man cave. (It was really a cave, too!) All he wanted to do was talk to me about his glory days fighting the Lamanites: "I once smote four Lamanites with a single smite!" he kept saying. It took all my patience not to say, "Sir, I'm here because I'm totally *smitten* with your daughter, not to hear about what a good smiter you were!"

Anyway, enjoy the chocolate milk, or donut, or green smoothie, or whatever it is you like. Personally, I like my green smoothies made with mint chocolate chip ice cream. As far as I'm concerned, if it's green, it's a vegetable. So, where were we? Oh, yes. My story. I guess we should move it along a bit. I'm thinking we've got about eight more minutes before someone casually begins to fold laundry near where you're sitting and nonchalantly asks you a question about what you're reading. And I'd rather not have your first answer be, "Captain Moroni drinks his green smoothies with ice cream." Yeah, that might undermine my reputation with your parental units, which would in turn negatively affect your chocolate milk consumption, and we don't want that, right?

So, have you ever wondered why there are so many chapters in the Book of Mormon about little old me? There were tons of wars between the Nephites and the Lamanites, and many chief captains. Why did the prophet Mormon choose to spend so much time on my fight against Amalickiah? Shoot, Mormon liked my story so much he even named his own son after me. You might remember him. He was the Moroni who appeared to Joseph Smith and gave him the golden plates. That's a totally different Moroni. Super cool guy, but not me. He's the one on top of the temples. They asked me if I wanted to be up there, but it turns out the statues would have been too top-heavy because of my massive pectorals. Also, I'm not very good on the trumpet. (I'm more of a trombone guy.)

Did you know Mormon saw your day? He saw the world you live in and the blessings and problems of the last days. Mormon said he couldn't write even a "hundredth part" of everything that came to pass in the Nephite civilization.[1] If you think about it, the Book of Mormon actually fast-forwards through a lot of the wars. This is especially true in the Book of Ether. There are some verses in Ether where it seems like they go from war back to peace back to war again four different times! In one verse! I'm like, whoa, slow down! I'm trying to catch up with who is smiting whom here!

Mormon was so careful about what he included in his summary *because* he saw your day. He saw planes and video games, texting, tweeting, and even man buns—don't get me started on man buns!

1. Words of Mormon 1:5.

Anyway, I believe there are many reasons Mormon was prompted to put so much of my story in the Book of Mormon, but there is one specific reason that I want to talk to you about today.

Temptation.

What does my war against Amalickiah have to do with temptation, you ask? Everything. You see, Amalickiah was prideful, Amalickiah was selfish, and Amalickiah was dishonest—just like sin and temptation. Basically, Amalickiah *is* temptation. And since my friends and I defeated Amalickiah with the help of the Lord in my day, I can give you a few pointers on how you can receive the Lord's help to defeat temptation in your day. As we go through life, we all experience temptation. Whatever kind of temptation you may be experiencing, here you will find tools to help you stay clean and pure. There is nothing so awesome as knowing you are clean before the Lord. Not even chocolate milk!

So soldier up, and let's take a little walk down memory lane. Well, not an actual walk—don't get up. It's an analogy, or a proverb . . . simile? I get all of those mixed up. Anyway, just listen up, Buttercup. Before you can really understand what a complete and total loser Amalickiah was, you need a little backstory. I guess you could call it my "origin" story . . .

CHAPTER 2

CAPTAIN MORONI'S ORIGIN STORY

A year or two before Amalickiah showed up in the Book of Mormon, I was named chief captain of the Nephite armies. The previous chief captain was a great leader named Zoram, who had two sons, Lehi and Aha. (Who names their kid Aha? Think about when he played hide-and-seek. . . . Whenever anyone found him they probably yelled, "A*ha*!" I imagine that got old for poor young Aha.)

My call as chief captain came as a bit of a surprise to everyone since I wasn't one of Zoram's sons, and I was only twenty-five years old at the time. Okay, yes, the paintings are accurate: I *was* pretty buff, but it takes more than brawn to defeat the Lamanites, alright?

I admit I was happy to be called as chief captain, but not because I wanted power. You see, I had an idea. The fact is, the Lamanites outnumbered us—by a lot. Like, *a lot* a lot. Nevertheless, we had been preserved by God for many years despite our small numbers. I believed that the harder we worked to help ourselves, the more God would help us. I didn't just want to *win* the wars, I wanted to reduce the number of dead—the number of Nephites *and* Lamanites we lost along the way.

So, drum roll, please . . . my big idea was to use armor! I know, I know, that doesn't sound like a big deal to you, Buttercup, but back in my day, no one was using armor among the Nephites or the Lamanites. In fact, the Lamanites would come to war in those silly little loincloth things. They thought it made them look scary, and they were right—just not in the way the Lamanites thought . . . gross!

I decided we didn't need to limit ourselves to just wearing thick clothing. Why not go really big and wear metal? You see, when Limhi's people showed up a while back, they didn't just bring back the plates of Ether. They brought back quite a few artifacts they discovered among the ruins of the Jaredite civilization. Some of it . . . well, some of it smelled pretty bad, I'm not going to lie! But some of it was really cool armor, unlike anything that had ever been used among the children of Lehi.

It's easy to get in the habit of doing the same things over and over again. Why not try new ideas? Once I became chief captain, I put our military R&D into overdrive. R&D is a cool way of saying "research and development."

We started developing new materials, testing them in all kinds of conditions, and generally going full James Bond long before James Bond was even born. Well, okay, I guess James Bond wasn't ever *born*, because he's not really real, but you know what I mean. What, Buttercup? Did I ruin that for you? Did you still believe in James Bond and the Easter Bunny? Sorry, not sorry. Santa, by the way, is totally real. Don't mess with Santa.

Anyway, we had a lot of success finding materials and armor that seemed promising, but frankly, I hoped we would never have to use them. Unfortunately, our opportunity for real battle testing came sooner than we'd all hoped.

Let me set the scene of this first big battle for you. As you might recall, Alma the Younger had been elected the first chief judge among the Nephites. After eight years, he left the judge's seat to teach the people. He felt like the best way to build a strong government was to help the people to gain a testimony of Jesus Christ, and then they would govern themselves. So at the time of this particular battle, Alma was not the chief judge anymore, but he was still the prophet.

Alma's teaching among the people had been very effective, whole cities were brought closer to the Lord. However, in the land of Zoram fewer people were converted, and the Zoramites who weren't converted decided to disagree disagreeably. You remember the Zoramites, right? The Rameumptom people? Seriously, what is the deal with the Rameumptom?! Climbing up a ladder to a small wooden stand and thanking God for making you so awesome and everyone else so lame? Who does that?! Well, the Zoramites did, until Alma showed up and converted half the city. Then the rest of them got mad and decided they wanted to destroy us.

Of *course* they did . . . because destroying people who want to help you makes sense?!

The Zoramites did what any dissenter does when they go cray-cray: they ran to the Lamanites for help. I tell you, when I think of how many wars were caused by Nephite dissenters scurrying over to the Lamanites, it makes me as tired as that whole "cray-cray" saying. Are you alright if we retire that one, Buttercup?

So the Zoramites ran to the Lamanites, and the Lamanites said, "Go fight the Nephites? Umm, let me think about it for three milliseconds—Okay, let's do it!" The leader of the Lamanite army was a guy named Zerahemnah (not to be confused with Zarahem-LA, the Nephite capital city). Zerahemnah immediately sent around a survey to all the Lamanite

soldiers that said something along the lines of, "On a scale of one to ten, with one being like a pebble stuck in your sandal and ten being like the burning heat of a thousand suns, how much do you hate the Nephites?" Zerahemnah then chose the Lamanites who most hated the Nephites to be his sub-captains. Great, just what we needed, super-caffeinated Lamanite hatred on steroids. Wonderful.[2]

While the Lamanites and Zoramites were fueling themselves with hatred, this is what the Book of Alma says about the Nephites at the time: "And now the design of the Nephites was to support their lands, and their houses, and their wives, and their children, that they might preserve them from the hands of their enemies; and also that they might preserve their rights and their privileges, yea, and also their liberty, that they might worship God according to their desires. For they knew that if they should fall into the hands of the Lamanites, that whosoever should worship God in spirit and truth, the true and the living God, the Lamanites would destroy."[3]

Yep, we were the good guys.

So once we found out the Lamanites were preparing for battle, I gave my troops their new uniforms—er, armor—and we went out to meet the Lamanites in battle. The Lamanites were dressed to kill in their, um, really *airy* loincloths (except for the dissenting Zoramites, who wore normal clothing—I guess even dissenters have standards, right?). And there *we* were, dressed to . . . well, dressed to *live*! The Lamanites took one look at us, and—*boom!*—their minds were blown! They were so shocked, you would have thought we were a herd of cureloms and cumoms (look 'em up). The Lamanites took off into the wilderness, scared witless. It was definitely a top-ten-plays kind of moment.

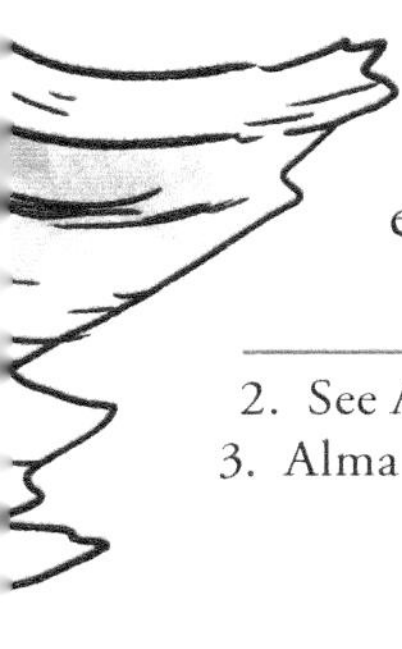

But I knew the moment wouldn't last. I was sure the Lamanites weren't going home, rather just going a different way. But which way? I decided to do what I always do:

2. See Alma 43:1–8.

3. Alma 43:9–10.

work like it all depends on me, and pray like it all depends on the Lord. I sent spies into the wilderness to follow the Lamanite army, and I sent messengers to the prophet Alma so he would pray and tell me where the Lord wanted us to go. The Lord told Alma we should go to the land of Manti, so that's what we did. Sure enough, that was exactly where the Lamanites were headed! Thanks to the Lord, we got there so early that we were able to set a trap for the Lamanites.

I commanded part of my army to hide on the east side of the river Sidon, and another part to hide on the west of the river. I was with one group, and I put Lehi in charge of the other group. Remember Lehi, the son of Zoram, the previous chief captain? Lehi was an amazing soldier, and everyone was pretty surprised when I was named the new chief captain instead of him. I admit, I was a little worried Lehi would feel upset, but I had nothing to worry about. Lehi accepted me as captain and became one of my best friends. Lehi wasn't worried about power; he was worried about righteousness. My kind of guy.

So Lehi's on one side of the river and I'm on the other, and his men are yelling, "East side!" and my men are yelling, "West side!" back and forth. "East side!" "West side!" It was pretty awesome. Just kidding. We were actually being super quiet like an elite team of Nephite ninjas, waiting for the Lamanites to enter the river's valley. *Ssshhh!*

After the Lamanites entered and moved past Lehi, he and his men jumped out and attacked their rear flank. The Lamanites turned to fight, but even though there were more Lamanites, several Lamanites fell for every one Nephite. As usual, the Lord was protecting us because of our righteousness, and now we had armor as well! Things were going better than ever. The Lamanites became frightened and began to flee across the river Sidon to the west side. Imagine the Lamanites' surprise when Lehi and his men didn't follow them but just stayed on the east side. Then imagine the Lamanites' even *greater* surprise when I jumped out of the woods with *my* men on the west side of the river! Let's just say that the Lamanites began to be very, very astonished!

First, they ran back toward the river, toward Lehi's men. Then, they ran back toward me and my men, and then back toward Lehi. Have you ever watched people who are watching a tennis match? Their heads go left, then to the right, then back to the left, and back again to the right? Yeah, it was like that, but with swords and cimeters instead of tennis rackets. So I guess not really that much like tennis at all . . . well, you get the picture.

We had the Lamanites surrounded, and they were not happy campers. In fact, they got so fired up by the hatred of their leaders that the book of Alma says, "Never had the Lamanites been known to fight with such exceedingly great strength and courage, no, not even from the beginning. . . . yea, they did fight like dragons, and many of the Nephites were slain by their hands, yea, for they did smite in two many of their head-plates, and they did pierce many of their breastplates, and they did smite off many of their arms; and thus the Lamanites did smite in their fierce anger."[4]

Yeah, I was there, and it's true, the Lamanites fought like they never had before, and we lost a lot of good men that day. But the Lamanites' hatred wasn't enough. You see, Alma also records, "Nevertheless, the Nephites were inspired by a better cause, for they were not fighting for monarchy nor power but they were fighting for their homes and their liberties, their wives and their children, and their all."[5]

Always remember: goodness is stronger fuel than hatred. It's easy to forget. In fact, during this battle, when my men saw the fierceness of the anger of the Lamanites, they were about to shrink and flee from them. I could see it starting to happen, so I began to inspire them as best I could. "Remember your wives!" I yelled. "Remember your children and your homes and your God! Remember our freedom!" The other Nephite captains joined in, reminding our men of why we were fighting, how much we had to gain, and how much we had to lose. And it worked! My men "turned upon the Lamanites, and they cried with one voice unto the Lord their God, for their liberty and their freedom from bondage."[6]

4. Alma 43:43–44.
5. Alma 43:45.
6. Alma 43:48–49.

The Lord heard our prayers, and He strengthened my men as a result. The Lamanites began to flee from us back toward the river. But when the Lamanites saw the men of Lehi on the east side of the river and my men and me on the west side, and that they were surrounded, they were struck with terror. I saw the terror in their eyes, and having seen the success of the first phase of my great idea—armor—now it was time to roll out phase two: mercy.

I commanded my men to stop fighting and to step back a bit. Then I looked at the captain of the Lamanites and gave such an awesome speech that Mormon included the whole thing in the golden plates, word for word. And that's saying a lot, considering I've given some pretty great speeches.

> Behold, Zerahemnah, that we do not desire to be men of blood. Ye know that ye are in our hands, yet we do not desire to slay you.
>
> Behold, we have not come out to battle against you that we might shed your blood for power; neither do we desire to put you into bondage. But this is the very cause for which ye have come against us; yea, and ye are angry with us because of our religion.
>
> But now, ye behold that the Lord is with us; and ye behold that he has delivered you into our hands. And now I would that ye should understand that this is done unto us because of our religion and our faith in Christ. And now ye see that ye cannot destroy this our faith.
>
> Now ye see that this is the true faith of God; yea, ye see that God will support and keep, and preserve us, so long as we are faithful unto him, and unto our faith, and our religion; and never will the Lord suffer that we shall be destroyed except we should fall into transgression and deny our faith.
>
> And now, Zerahemnah, I command you, in the name of that all-powerful God, who has strengthened our arms that we have gained power over you, by our faith, by our religion, and by our rites of worship, and by our church, and by the sacred support which we owe to our wives and our children, by that liberty which binds us to our lands and our country; yea, and also by the maintenance of the sacred word of God, to which we owe all our happiness; and by all that is most dear to us—
>
> Yea, and this is not all; I command you by all the desires which ye have for life, that ye deliver up your weapons of war unto us, and

> we will seek not your blood, but we will spare your lives, *if ye will go your way and come not again to war against us.*[7]

That last line was the key to everything. Would the Lamanites be willing to promise never to attack us again if we let them live? It was the million-onti question.

There was a pause as the Lamanites all considered my offer. It was a new one, that's for sure. It was new to them, and it was new to my men. I could tell that some of my men were surprised as well.

I went on, "And now, if ye do not this, behold, ye are in our hands, and I will command my men that they shall fall upon you, and inflict the wounds of death in your bodies, that ye may become extinct; and then we will see who shall have power over this people; yea, we will see who shall be brought into bondage."[8]

I wanted to make it very clear to them what was being offered. If they were unwilling to promise never to fight again, I could not let them go. Why let them go just to see them fight another day? We had them surrounded *now*, so if they were planning to just come back and fight again, no thank you, we'll just end it now.

Finally, Zerahemnah stepped forward and set his sword and his cimeter and his bow in front of me. It seemed like my plan was working, and I began to feel very hopeful. However, there was something about Zerahemnah's look that didn't quite say "full surrender." I soon understood why, as he said, "Behold, here are our weapons of war; we will deliver them up unto you, but we will not suffer ourselves to take an oath unto you, which we know that we shall break, and also our children; but take our weapons of war, and suffer that we may depart into the wilderness; otherwise we will retain our swords, and we will perish or conquer!"[9]

There is a lot going on here in Zerahemnah's speech, Buttercup, so pay attention. First of all, he set down his weapons, but he didn't give his word that they wouldn't fight again. Why not? Why not

7. Alma 44:1–6, emphasis added.
8. Alma 44:7.
9. Alma 44:8.

make a fake promise not to fight in the future and then ignore that promise and come back later and fight anyway? These are evil Lamanites, right? Don't they lie, cheat, and steal all the time? What's the big deal with breaking an oath?

Actually, oaths and promises *were* a big deal to the Lamanites. Just because they had been taught for generations that the Nephites were bad doesn't mean that the Lamanites were completely evil. Remember how Jacob taught that the Lamanites loved their wives and their children, and that they were doing better in that way than the Nephites? Remember when Ammon and his brothers baptized thousands of Lamanites? I sure remember; those conversions happened when I was a small boy. I still remember my parents voting to accept the Anti-Nephi-Lehites and to give them the land of Jershon by the seashore. Good people, my parents.

I suspected for a long time that because the Lamanites were still descendants of Lehi, because they still had the light of Christ, perhaps many of them would respond favorably to mercy. Perhaps, just perhaps, they would be willing to make a promise not to come back and fight. This battle was the test. Even though Zerahemnah's initial response indicated that he was unwilling to make an oath, it still confirmed an important part of my theory: Lamanites take their promises seriously. Even Zerahemnah didn't

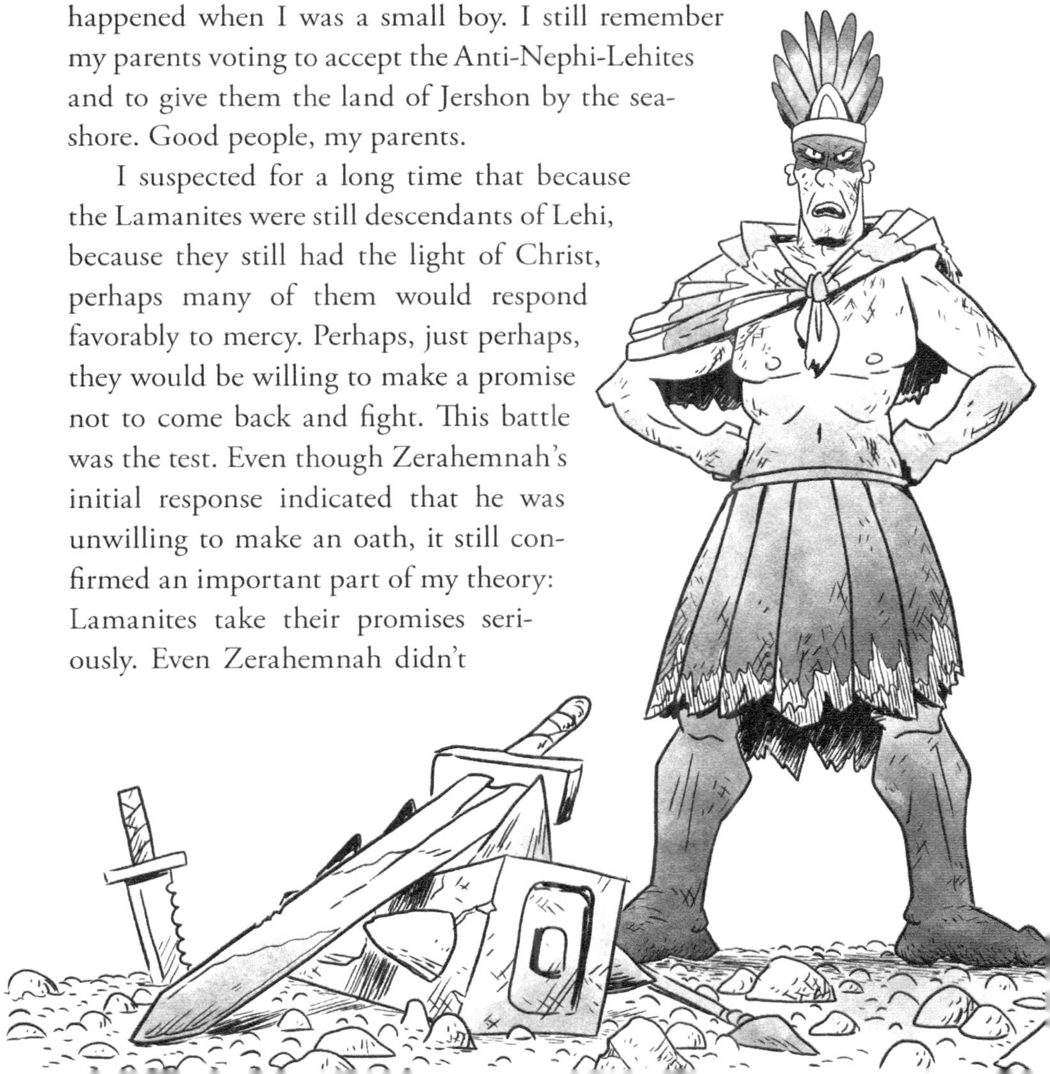

want to make a promise he thought he might break. To me, this was encouraging.

Zerahemnah went on, "Behold, we are not of your faith; we do not believe that it is God that has delivered us into your hands; but we believe that it is your cunning that has preserved you from our swords. Behold, it is your breastplates and your shields that have preserved you."[10]

Boom! Now it was *my* mind that was blown! *Our armor? That's why Zerahemnah thinks we have been preserved?! Really?!* Now, I readily admit that the armor helped—that's why I wanted it in the first place—but I couldn't help thinking Zerahemnah had a really short memory! At the time of this battle, the Nephites and Lamanites had been in the Americas for over 515 years, during which the Nephites had been outnumbered in every. single. war! Almost all of which, by the way, the Nephites had won. So notwithstanding over 500 years of outnumbered, armorless victories, *today*, just because we have armor *today*, Zerahemnah says our victory is solely because of our *armor*?! What about the fact that we just happened to be hiding right where the Lamanites were traveling? How is it that we were in the exact right spot hours before the Lamanites got here?! Because of Alma's revelation, that's how! Don't get me wrong, I am grateful for the armor, but I never pretended that armor alone was enough. The protection of the Lord is everything.

I didn't say all this to Zerahemnah. I knew he wouldn't listen. I wasn't angry as much as I was saddened by his stubbornness. I pulled myself together and said, "I cannot recall the words which I have spoken, therefore as the Lord liveth, ye shall not depart except ye depart with an oath that ye will not return against us to war. Now as ye are in our hands we will spill your blood upon the ground, or ye shall submit to the conditions which I have proposed."[11] I wish you could have been there and seen it. I wish you could have heard me. I was emotional. I could see there were

10. Alma 44:9.
11. Alma 44:11.

a lot of Lamanites who disagreed with Zerahemnah, who seemed willing to accept my offer. Some of them, sure, some of them just wanted to live. But I could see that others "got it." They got what I was trying to do, they got that we didn't want to kill them, that we didn't hate them. I could see many of them looking thoughtful, as if re-evaluating everything they had been taught about us, all the lies they had been told about the Nephites. And as I spoke, I looked at those whom I could see responding positively, trying to communicate my heart through my eyes.

Well, I know now that I probably shouldn't have taken my eyes off of Zerahemnah! He took advantage of the change in mood, the slackening muscles, the emotion of my appeal, and he grabbed his sword off the ground and lunged at me!

Fortunately, I wasn't alone. One of my soldiers was ready. As Zerahemnah raised his sword, my buddy Teancum raised his own sword and hit Zerahemnah's sword so hard that he broke it at the hilt. Then, in a flash, he sliced Zerahemnah across the scalp, cutting

a large stretch of skin and hair off of Zerahemnah's head, without breaking his skull.

Everyone gasped, Zerahemnah ran and hid in the crowd of his men, and I smiled at Teancum and said, "That was tight, like unto a dish!"

Then, Teancum picked up Zerahemnah's scalp with the point of his sword, lifted it into the air, and said in a loud voice, "Even as this scalp has fallen to the earth, which is the scalp of your chief, so shall ye fall to the earth except ye will deliver up your weapons of war and depart with a covenant of peace."[12]

At first, nobody moved. Then one Lamanite soldier stepped forward, dropped his weapons at my feet, looked me full in the face, and said in a strong, loud voice, "My name is Lehonti, and I am a Lamanite. I am not afraid to die, but I do not believe that you came here today to kill me, or any of us. I now covenant with thee that I will never return to fight the Nephites, as long as you leave my family and people in peace. But if you should ever come to *our* land to attack *us* . . ."—and here he turned around and spoke to his fellow Lamanites, slowly and meaningfully—"which the Nephites have *never done before* . . ." He paused for effect, and then turned back to me and said, "Then I will defend myself and my family to the death."

I was floored. It was like I was dreaming. I could not imagine a better response. Lehonti's words drove my point home stronger than I ever could have alone. We, the Nephites, were not the aggressors. *Nor had we ever been!* Surely some Lamanites must have noticed that we were never bringing the fight to them. Well, Lehonti clearly noticed, and he made sure his comrades noticed too. He also made sure everyone knew he wasn't surrendering due to fear or weakness. Goodness is never weakness.

Many others followed Lehonti's example, dropping their weapons and entering into a covenant of peace. I could tell it wasn't easy for them. If looks could kill, they would each have suffered

12. Alma 44:15.

a thousand deaths as they broke from their kinsmen and came forward to enter into the covenant. Many of the Lamanites were angry with those who were leaving and were clearly not about to join them.

Finally, before any more could leave, Zerahemnah began to scream at those whom he termed traitors, "and he did stir up the remainder of his soldiers to anger, to contend more powerfully against the Nephites."[13]

Zerahemnah certainly ruined the moment. I was sure that if he had just kept quiet, many others would have come forward as well. Zerahemnah's bullheadedness really ticked me off and left me no other choice than to command my men to renew the battle.

But the Lamanite forces were depleted, and many of their hearts were not in it. Furthermore, they were just as unprotected as before, dressed only in their wispy little loincloths. It saddens me to report that the Lamanites began to fall exceedingly fast before the swords of my men. "They began to be swept down," just like Teancum had prophesied when he lifted Zerahemnah's scalp upon his sword.[14]

13. Alma 44:16.
14. Alma 44:18.

Finally, seeing that he and his men were about to perish, Zerahemnah yelled out to me, promising that he would covenant, and also his people with him, never to come to war against the Nephites if we would spare their lives.

Once again, I called off my men, and we withdrew a pace from the Lamanites. After requiring each of them to individually turn in their weapons and enter into a covenant of peace, we allowed them to depart into the wilderness.

My men were jubilant! My plan, in their minds, had worked. And while I knew I probably should also have felt happy, as I looked around on the greatness of the number of dead, of both the Nephites and the Lamanites, happiness was not my strongest emotion.

So many men died that day, we didn't count the bodies. As I helped my men cast the dead into the River Sidon, to meander their way to the depths of the sea, I tried to console myself with the thought of those Lamanites returning to their land, carrying a promise never to fight us again.[15]

Could it be true? No more wars? Oh, how I hoped it were true! And it might have been . . . if not for Amalickiah.

My men and I returned to Zarahemla as heroes. While everyone was accustomed to defeating the Lamanites, they were shocked at the manner of the victory. The armor had worked better than anyone hoped, and everyone was floored that the Lamanites had entered into a covenant of peace. The record states, "Behold, now it came to pass that the people of Nephi were exceedingly rejoiced, because the Lord had again delivered them out of the hands of their enemies; therefore they gave thanks unto the Lord their God; yea, and they did fast much and pray much, and they did worship God with exceedingly great joy."[16]

Did you know that you could fast in gratitude? Usually, we fast for special blessings on behalf of ourselves or for others. But if you

15. Alma 44:21.
16. Alma 45:1.

think about it, a fast is like a twenty-four-hour-long prayer. Prayer is a form of work, an exercise in faith. The whole time we are not eating during a fast, we are also showing our faith, making fasting like a supercharged prayer. Because of the additional sacrifice of food and drink, fasting can make available blessings that may not come by prayer alone. When we pray, we give thanks for our blessings and request additional blessings. Fasting is no different. We can give thanks as well as ask for blessings. Too often we only ask for blessings when we fast.

We Nephites would often fast in thanksgiving. Now, I'm not telling you to fast *on* Thanksgiving, that beautiful holiday you get to enjoy every November. No, I'm just saying that sometimes you can actually fast and tell Heavenly Father that you are so thankful for a particular blessing or blessings you have received, that you are not asking for anything during your fast, but only fasting *in* thanksgiving.

All this talk of Thanksgiving is making me hungry! I can't wait to eat some cranberry sauce! Just kidding! Cranberry sauce?! No one looks forward to *cranberry sauce*, am I right?! I'm a two-fisted turkey leg kind of guy myself. One in each hand.

Like I said, you don't have to fast on Thanksgiving, but you may decide to fast in gratitude for particular blessings you or others in your life have received. I happen to have it on very good authority that Heavenly Father really appreciates it when we fast in gratitude.

Did you know you can also fast if you are mourning? Unfortunately, we Nephites had a lot of experience mourning, and often fasted when our loved ones had been killed in war.[17] Fasting brings us closer to the Spirit, and the Spirit is awesome at comforting those who are mourning. If you ever experience something very sad in your life, you can fast for comfort, and the Spirit will be there for you. I know fasting brings peace.

But . . . you aren't fasting right now! And it's been a while since your last chocolate milk refill, so let out another sigh of

17. Helaman 9:10

exasperation, stretch a bit, maybe wipe your brow with your sleeve, and then . . . say it with me: "Mom? Could I maybe have a bit more chocolate milk? I've been reading for a while now, and Moroni hasn't even started talking about Amalickiah yet . . ."

Ahh yeah! Watch the chocolate milk flow like the River Sidon!

Hey, Buttercup, could you bring me a green smoothie with a sprig of parsley? And Buttercup, when I say "green smoothie," I mean "chocolate milkshake," and when I say "sprig of parsley," I mean "dollop of whipped cream."

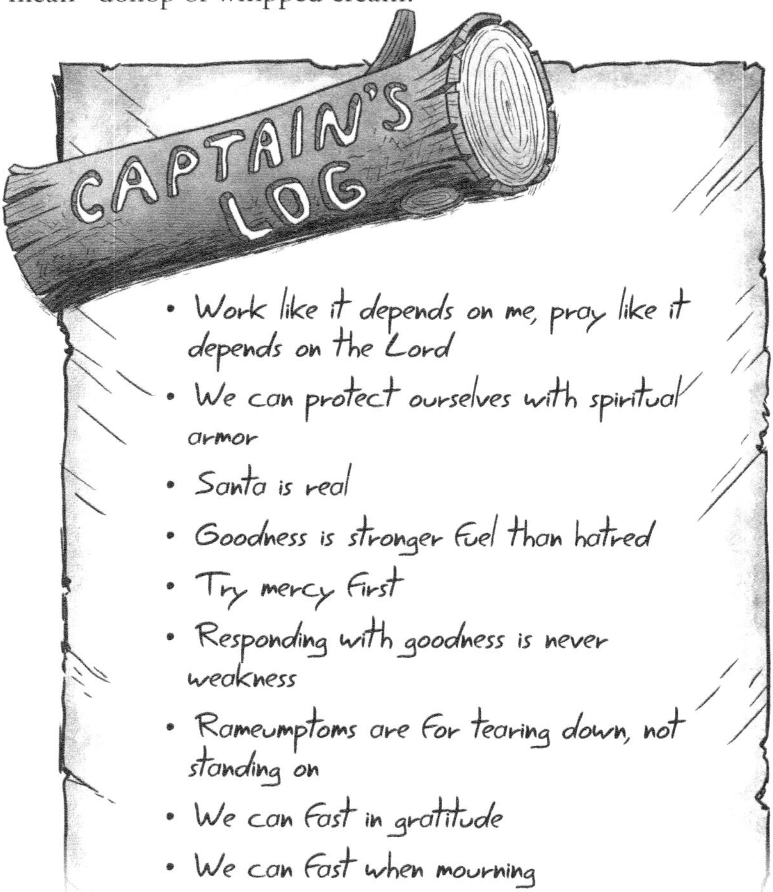

CHAPTER 3

AMALICKIAH'S ESCAPE

Alright, now on to Amalickiah!

After defeating the Lamanites, I thought we'd get home from the war to find everyone so happy! Finally, a little bit of peace! And most people were thankful, but not Amalickiah. Frankly, I think part of his problem was that he was bored. He thought he was pretty smart, and rather than use his intelligence to help others, he decided to use it to help himself—to help himself to whatever he wanted. Remember this, my friends: boredom is very powerful. It can lead to great goodness or great wickedness. Every time you are bored, you get to choose. The adversary will try to take advantage of your boredom and tempt you to fill it with the wrong kinds of things.

I'm not sure how much "well-doing" Amalickiah was involved in before he attempted to take over the world, but he had certainly become weary of it. And he was not interested in taking direction from anyone. Soon after the battle, Alma entrusted the records—and the position of high priest and prophet—to his son Helaman. Not everyone was happy with Helaman's calling. They questioned whether Helaman had been chosen by God. Amalickiah was one of the lower judges, and he and some of his fellow judges decided not to listen to Helaman. The record states, "They grew proud, being lifted up in their hearts, because of their exceedingly great riches; therefore they grew rich in their own eyes, and would not give heed to [Helaman's] words, to walk uprightly before God."[18]

For hundreds of years, kings had ruled the Nephites, and some Nephites still preferred having a king over having judges. Amalickiah thought that *he* should be king, and he promised many of the lower judges that if they helped him become king, he would give them more power. Amalickiah and his followers didn't want to help the people; they wanted to help themselves. They were proud and selfish.

So there I was, sitting at home a short time after the successful battle with the Lamanites, relaxing with my family. I was watching my two sons playing together, acting out the fight with Zerahemnah. They kept switching back and forth between pretending to be Zerahemnah and pretending to be Teancum. They didn't ever want to pretend to be me. "Mercy is *so* not cool, Dad!" they kept telling me.

The next thing I knew, the real Teancum marched into my house, signed my kids' foam cimeters, and then told me about Amalickiah's plot to become king of the Nephites. Boy, did that tick me off! (If I had known how to turn into a giant, muscular, green guy, I totally would have! Of course, considering I already have massive muscles, I guess I'd only have to turn green. **wink**)

Right then and there, I grabbed my coat, ripped it in half, and wrote, "In memory of our God, our religion, and our freedom and our wives and our children."[19] I threw on my armor, and instead of turning green, I knelt down and began to pray. I prayed

18. Alma 45:24.
19. Alma 46:12.

mightily to God for the blessings of liberty to rest upon me and my people, so long as there should a band of Christians remain on the land.[20]

When I stood up, I felt encouraged by the Spirit, and I said, "Surely God shall not suffer that we, who are despised because we take upon us the name of Christ, shall be trodden down and destroyed, until we bring it upon us by our own transgressions."[21] Then I ran out of the house to the central square of Zarahemla, waving the torn part of my coat in the air, that all might see the writing. I yelled out with a loud voice, saying, "Behold, whosoever will maintain this title upon the land, let them come forth in the strength of the Lord, and enter into a covenant that they will maintain their rights, and their religion, that the Lord God may bless them."[22]

Then I just stood there. Waiting. I honestly didn't know how the people were going to react. A lot of people left, quickly. I thought maybe Amalickiah had already gotten to them. Maybe the Nephites actually wanted a jerk like that for a king. Or maybe they all thought I'd gone loco. I didn't know, so I just stood there looking around awkwardly. Suddenly people started running toward me with their armor on. *This is it*, I thought. *They're done with me. They don't like me anymore, and they are going to kill me or haul me off to prison.*

But I was wrong.

The people with their armor were also holding a shirt or coat like mine, and they were running up to me, ripping the garments they were holding, and then throwing them at my feet. The pile got bigger and bigger around my feet, and so did the crowd around me. The first one to me, by the way, was Lehi.

It probably sounds weird that they would rip a shirt to show their support, but think of it like a "high five" or a "fist bump" back in my day. The Nephites were tearing up old shirts as a kind

20. Alma 46:13.
21. Alma 46:18.
22. Alma 46:20.

of covenant or promise that they would support God, liberty, and little old me. I thought this was pretty awesome, actually. I became confident that more Nephites would feel the same way, so I sent letters to my friends in every Nephite city, inviting all the people who wanted to maintain their liberty and stand against Amalickiah and his dissenters to enter into the same covenant. The results were overwhelmingly positive.

Guess who noticed? Yep, Amalickiah. I guess you could say he realized his election polls were falling fast. Some of his "friends" started to get cold feet, too. They began to doubt Amalickiah, to question his motives. So he fled. Amalickiah took whoever would go with him and—you guessed it: he tried to run to the Lamanites to get their help! Arrgh!

Well, as glad as I was to see Amalickiah gone, I didn't think it was a good idea to just let him and his followers go and try to stir up the Lamanites. We had just completed a war with the Lamanites, and I wasn't interested in jumping right back into another one just because Amalickiah was bored and power-hungry.

So I took off after them with my army. The good news is that we caught them . . . the bad news is that Amalickiah and a handful of his men got away.

CHAPTER 4

AMALICKIAH IS NEVER #2

When we got back to Zarahemla, a lot of people were rejoicing. Amalickiah was gone, and the Lamanite army had promised not to come back and fight us. What could go wrong? But I wasn't convinced. For some reason, I just couldn't imagine Amalickiah settling down in a quiet Lamanite farming village, giving up on his aspirations for world domination.

I could have relaxed, and a lot of people told me that I should. But I had a feeling Amalickiah was keeping busy, and I knew boredom led to either goodness or wickedness, so I chose to keep busy doing good.

I'm glad I did.

Not long after Amalickiah escaped, we began receiving odd reports from our spies along the borders with the Lamanites. First, the Lamanite king ordered his army into battle against us. Then we heard the army refused and fled to where the Lamanites kept their weapons. I was so happy! The Lamanite soldiers were keeping their promise! But then, just a short time later, we received a report that there was a new king of the Lamanites.

And his name was Amalickiah! Whaaaa?!

There were a lot of shocked people among the Nephites, but I was not one of them. It's important that you understand how Amalickiah became king of the Lamanites, and I have to admit that if I hadn't seen it happen, I wouldn't believe it myself.

As I suspected, Amalickiah didn't retire to a quiet life of farming after he fled into the wilderness. Instead, he went straight to the king of the Lamanites and told him he'd been one of the lower judges of the Nephites. Amalickiah told the king lies about the Nephites, lies about Helaman, lies about the chief judge, and lies about me. Amalickiah told the king, "*You* should be king over *all* the land, and many Nephites agree!" Amalickiah flattered the king and told him that my army had only won the last battle because of our armor and thick clothing. Amalickiah said he could help the king outfit the Lamanite army even better and defeat the Nephites. Amalickiah used the king's pride and selfishness against him. And the king fell for it.

Almost immediately, the king ordered his army to prepare for war against the Nephites. Imagine his surprise when most of them said no! (I still wish I could have seen his face!) The Lamanite army had not only just been defeated by my Nephite army, but they had also all just promised they would never fight us again. Most of them kept their promise and said no to the king! Well, the king didn't like that very much, so he gave Amalickiah command of those soldiers who were willing to fight the Nephites and told him to take them and force the others to fight.

The Lamanites who didn't want to fight fled to Mount Antipas. Nearby was Onidah, where the Lamanite army kept all their weapons. I know, right? The weapons armory is a super smart place to flee to! Not only were these promise keepers smart, but they were also committed. They were "fixed in their minds with a determined resolution that they would not be subjected to go against the Nephites."[23] They named themselves a leader: Lehonti.

23. Alma 47:6.

You remember Lehonti, right? He was the first Lamanite to have entered into a covenant of peace back at the River Sidon. Lehonti earned a lot of respect that day in the battlefield. Man, I loved that guy!

Amalickiah, now at the head of half the Lamanite army, led the way to Mount Antipas and had his men camp at the bottom of the mountain. When night fell, he sent his most trusted servant (a fellow Nephite by birth) up to Lehonti's camp to ask Lehonti to come down and meet with Amalickiah at the bottom of the hill. Lehonti refused. Smart man!

Amalickiah sent his servant up once again to ask Lehonti to come down. Again, Lehonti refused. A third time, Amalickiah asked Lehonti to come down to meet, and for the third time, Lehonti refused. Finally, Amalickiah went up the mountain himself, asked Lehonti to come outside and meet him, and even told Lehonti he could bring his guards with him. Lehonti had been so strong up to this point. He had kept his promise not to fight the Nephites, he had led the others to Onidah, the place of weapons, and he had refused to give in to Amalickiah's tricks. Surely Lehonti would stay strong now!

But he didn't. I don't know why Lehonti gave in. Maybe he thought "just this once" he would be safe. Maybe he thought if he talked to Amalickiah with his friends and bodyguards around him, it would be safe. Maybe he was just tired. Amalickiah had been working on Lehonti all night. Maybe Lehonti was just too tired to fight the temptation any longer, too tired to fight curiosity. Well, whatever the reason, Lehonti agreed to come outside and meet Amalickiah, and we all suffered because of it.

Once Amalickiah had Lehonti in front of him, he used the same tactics he had against the king of the Lamanites. Amalickiah used pride, selfishness, and deception. He flattered Lehonti, telling Lehonti that he was smart to stand up against the Lamanite king and not fight the Nephites. He reminded Lehonti that the Lamanite king often didn't even go out to war himself and wasn't a good leader. Amalickiah told Lehonti that *Lehonti* should be king, that he deserved it, and that a lot of people in the Lamanite cities felt the same way. Amalickiah said that he would allow Lehonti's men to come down and surround the rest of the Lamanite army in the night—and all Lehonti had to do was to make Amalickiah second in command.

My friends, temptation offers you glamour and power. It feeds your pride and your selfishness. Even good people like Lehonti can be brought down by pride and selfishness—especially late at night. Temptation lies to you, telling you that you are #1, that you deserve all your dreams and desires. Temptation tells you that it is more than happy to help you become #1, that it has no problem being #2 in your life. And temptation will come knocking as long and as late as you will allow it. But, like Amalickiah, temptation lies. Amalickiah was not willing to be #2 to anyone, and neither is temptation. Temptation is not happy to be #2 to you, to the Church, to your future eternal companion, to anyone. Temptation, like Amalickiah, only wants to be #1, and it will fight for the #1 spot if you give in to it. Temptation takes many forms, but whatever particular temptation you allow to overcome you, by it you will be brought into bondage.[24] Remember, there is a big difference between being tempted and giving in to temptation. Satan will try to tempt us with things our whole lives, but that doesn't mean we have to give in. Temptation only has power once we give in to it. Never convince yourself that giving in just a little is okay. Temptation has a way of quickly growing beyond whatever boundaries you might try to set for it. It will always work to become #1.

24. 2 Peter 2:19.

That's what we learn from Lehonti's story. You see, Lehonti gave in to Amalickiah little by little. First, Lehonti made a seemingly safe decision to come outside late at night "just this once" to meet Amalickiah while protected by his own guards. Then he made the seemingly wise and powerful decision to "just this once" accept Amalickiah's invitation to come down and surround the rest of the Lamanite army. Sure enough, Amalickiah kept his word, and after the surrounded Lamanites pled with Amalickiah to grant them their lives and to surrender to Lehonti, Amalickiah graciously agreed. Lehonti, in what he pretends to be a sign of reconciliation and generosity, then makes Amalickiah his right-hand man. Just. This. Once.

In the days that followed, I can only imagine the conversations between Amalickiah and Lehonti. Amalickiah continued to extol Lehonti's abilities, telling him how wise he was to resist the king, how much better of a leader he is than the king of the Lamanites, and how famous he is among the Nephites. While I can only imagine Amalickiah's lying words to Lehonti, I don't have to imagine what Amalickiah *did* to Lehonti.

Amalickiah poisoned Lehonti. Amalickiah told his closest servant to administer a small amount of poison to Lehonti's food. Just a little bit every day. Lehonti began to feel sick. It didn't seem to be anything serious, and no one assumed it was. Amalickiah expressed what appeared to be genuine concern right from the beginning. He took great pains to show this concern in front of others, appearing to take every precaution for Lehonti's health and safety. Lehonti received the best treatment available—and another small dose of poison with every meal. Eventually, this led to Lehonti's death. What Lehonti didn't understand is that when Amalickiah is #2, you are never #1. Amalickiah was like a poison everywhere he went. He tried to poison the government of the Nephites, he tried to poison the Lamanites and their promises not to fight, and he actually did poison Lehonti. Giving in to temptation acts much the same way as poison. Small doses may not seem to cause much harm, but taken repeatedly, it takes you away from God's plan for your life. Lehonti gave in to Amalickiah in small, seemingly safe doses. And, all at once, Lehonti was dead.

Upon Lehonti's death, the soldiers rallied around Amalickiah. They had seen his care for Lehonti, his concern for Lehonti's welfare. Amalickiah won the hearts of the army with his lying words and his subtle craftiness to do evil.

But Amalickiah wasn't finished. You see, he was now #1 with the army, but he was still #2 to the king of the Lamanites. Being #2 was never enough for Amalickiah. It took time, but he soon convinced his army that they needed to go back to the kingdom, and go back to the king. Unbeknownst to his men, Amalickiah sent an emissary to the king telling him that he had successfully defeated the leader of the rebellion, and that the army was reunited, ready to return, and raring to go destroy the Nephites! Of course, this wasn't true: many of the Lamanite soldiers still wanted to keep their covenant of peace. But the Lamanite king didn't know that, and so he was overjoyed by Amalickiah's letter of lies. So pleased was the king, he wrote back and told Amalickiah to return immediately and that the king himself would come out to greet them.

Amalickiah then doubled-down on his lies and told his men that the king had softened his stance, that he wasn't interested in fighting the Nephites anymore, and that he would be welcoming them back with open arms. "He's even coming out to meet us! Can you believe it?!"

Everyone felt like they were getting exactly what they wanted. But, as usual, only Amalickiah was getting what he wanted: to be #1.

On the appointed day, the king left the capital city with a handful of servants and went out to meet his army and his new #2 man, Amalickiah. How smart the king must have felt, sending Amalickiah to do his dirty work. How wonderfully his plan was working! How lucky to have Amalickiah on his side! The king had no idea how wrong he was.

Amalickiah sent his most faithful servants ahead to greet the king, well out of eyesight of the rest of the army. As they approached the king and his retinue, Amalickiah's servants bowed themselves before the king, as if to reverence him because of his greatness. The king put forth his hand to raise them, as a token of peace, and when he had raised the first servant from the ground—the same servant who poisoned Lehonti—that servant immediately lunged forward and stabbed the king in the heart. Just like Lehonti, the Lamanite king learned that you are never #1 when you've made Amalickiah #2. Amalickiah was never anyone's servant, and neither is sin. Sin is the master, and it uses pride, selfishness, and deceit to enslave and to kill, just like Amalickiah.

Boy, am I getting tired of talking about Amalickiah! He left a wake of destruction everywhere he went. Lehonti's death really gets to me. What a great man Lehonti was! First, Lehonti defied Zerahemnah and then the Lamanite king. He did this based only on his commitment to his principles. How I loved that man! If only Lehonti hadn't given in to temptation! Frankly, he should have just gone to bed earlier! He rejected Amalickiah several times but gave in late at night. Temptation doesn't give up, never closes, and will knock on your door 24/7. The longer and later you stand at the door and wonder if you should open it, the more likely you are to do so. Remember Lehonti, my friends, and don't put yourself in temptation's path late at night. When you're tired, your defenses are down and you're more susceptible.

Buttercup, do you mind if I change the subject for a minute? Talking about Amalickiah can be depressing. Can we talk about puppies or unicorns or something? Why don't you go grab the computer and pull up the latest crazy cat video. I could sure go for a crazy cat video right now! We didn't have crazy cat videos when I was growing up, because, well, we didn't have, you know, *video*. What we did have was surprise midnight jaguar attacks. Not quite the same, really. Sure, everyone talked about the jaguar attacks when they happened, but they didn't get many "likes."

Sometimes—**sigh**—I used to imagine Amalickiah having a late-night run-in with a jaguar. A guy can dream, can't he?

CHAPTER 5

AMALICKIAH BECOMES KING OF THE LAMANITES

Alright, alright, alright. Where was I? Oh yes, Amalickiah's servant had just stabbed the Lamanite king. Well, the murderer and his friends then turned on the king's servants, who took off into the wilderness, running for their lives. This was actually Amalickiah's plan all along, because once the king's servants ran, Amalickiah's servants began to yell, saying, "Behold, the servants of the king have stabbed the king to the heart, and he has fallen and they have fled; behold, come and see!"[25]

Hearing this, Amalickiah (good guy that he was—**retch**) commanded his army to march quickly to the spot of the murder. When they found the king lying there dead, Amalickiah pretended to be angry and said: "Whosoever loved the king, let him go forth, and pursue his servants that they may be slain!"[26] A host of Lamanites took off after the king's servants, but the servants were too fast and ran straight to Zarahemla to tell us what had happened.

When the Lamanite army returned, Amalickiah was ready for the next phase of his plan. He had killed the king, and next he took the Lamanite armies and took possession of their capital city, named the city of Nephi.[27] Although he now had control of the entire Lamanite army, he was still a Nephite by birth. Amalickiah

---

25. Alma 47:26.
26. Alma 47:27.
27. Alma 47:31.

was no idiot; he knew most Lamanites would not be very excited to have a Nephite-born king. He needed more legitimacy in order to truly gain the allegiance of the people, and he had an idea about how to get it. Yep, you guessed it! By flattery, selfishness, and deceit! You're really picking up on this!

Amalickiah sent a letter to the queen, telling her his own fabricated version of how the king died. She wrote back, first asking him to spare the city, and also asking him to come see her and bring witnesses of the killing. This was just what he wanted. Amalickiah took the same servant who had killed the king, and all those who were with him, "and went in unto the queen, unto the place where she sat; and they all testified unto her that the king was slain by his own servants; and they said also: They have fled; does not this testify against them? And thus they satisfied the queen concerning the death of the king."[28]

Was she really satisfied, though? The queen must have thought it odd to have all these Nephite dissenters testifying to her about the death of her husband. Surely she must have been suspicious. Amalickiah may have sensed her unease, so he began to flirt with the queen, the very woman whose husband he had just killed. He told her that he was just a simple Nephite who had no idea how to govern such a large group of people as the Lamanites. He flattered her, telling her that it was clear that she had always been the brains behind the Lamanites, and not her husband.

28. Alma 47:34.

He talked of being lonely and unaccustomed to the wealth of a king. Perhaps she could show him how to enjoy the finer things of life?

Amalickiah had already taken possession of the city. He could have killed the queen or exiled her and installed himself as the new king by force. However, doing so would not have endeared him to the Lamanites. Amalickiah knew he needed broad Lamanite support in order to mount an effective offensive against the Nephites, so by offering the queen continued power and wealth as his wife, Amalickiah was angling for greater legitimacy. Like her husband and Lehonti, the queen fell for Amalickiah's flattery. They were soon married.

Puppy! Quick, someone bring me a cute, cuddly little puppy! I am seriously about to lose my lunch, and all that, er . . . "green smoothie" I had earlier! Amalickiah's lying and scheming ways make me sick! But I can't stop my story now. There is something very important going on here, something you need to understand.

Do you see how thoughtful Amalickiah has been? I don't mean thoughtful in a "kind" and "caring" sort of way, but in a detailed and plotting way. Amalickiah hated the Nephites so much that he was willing to slowly and carefully do everything in his power to destroy us. He was willing to come up with a plan and take the time necessary to let it develop. This is what Satan does. Satan hates Heavenly Father so much that he is willing to take all the time necessary to slowly and carefully lead us down to hell.

Satan isn't going to beat down your front door with sin. No. He tempts you through those you thought were your friends. He entices you with little acts of dishonesty or selfishness. He's going to wait off to the side or bottom of your computer screen, near the crazy cat videos. You'll see a little video there on the side, with people who look just a bit alluring. Satan knows that early in the day, you'll probably ignore that alluring video. But, as the time gets later, and the cat videos less interesting, he knows that your eyes will wander back to that enticing video again. Finally, if it gets late enough, you might just click on it. That video may not be too bad, but it takes you away from safety. And there, away from safety, once again on the side or on the bottom of the computer screen, are more videos, each a little bit worse than the last. Soon, after only two or three clicks, you are far from safety.

But there is a way to prevent this. Satan isn't the only one who can plan. In fact, he stole the idea of planning in the first place. The original planner was Heavenly Father, and the original plan was the plan of salvation. And who is the central part of that plan? Yes, Jesus Christ! No one knows what it's like to be a part of a plan better than Jesus Christ. Did you know that by making Jesus Christ the central part of *His* plan, Heavenly Father was setting an example for us all? God knows that if we follow His example and build all our plans around Christ, *we will not fail*!

You can plan now to avoid and reject temptation. You can predecide how you will respond to temptation. What if someone offers you alcohol? How will you say no? Many people think they'll be offered drugs by some scary-looking gangster in a dark alley in the middle of the night. First of all, don't go to dark alleys in the middle of the night! Second, it is much more likely you will be offered drugs by an acquaintance somewhere you'd least expect it, like the hallway of your school. So plan ahead! If someone offers you drugs, you could give them a quick hug and then smile and say, "Hugs, not drugs," as you walk away. Not only is that hilarious, but it makes it clear that you are not at all interested.

The point is that if you don't decide how you are going to respond to temptation before temptation is on your doorstep, you're making things more difficult than they need to be. Remember to build your plan around Christ, and then it will be easy to turn down any temptation in the moment.

Even though Amalickiah built his plans around himself instead of Christ, he was willing to slowly and carefully bring them to pass. Do we love Heavenly Father enough to be willing to plan for our own righteousness? Do we love Heavenly Father enough to slowly and carefully help bring others unto Christ? We can't beat people up with righteousness, but we can soften their hearts with love and preparation.

Amalickiah also believed in preparation, but he relied on hate rather than love. Once he married the queen, he rolled out the next phase of his plan: propaganda. He had been among the Lamanite army long enough to know that their level of hatred toward the Nephites was at an all-time low. That would not do. You see, the Lamanite kingdom was not enough for Amalickiah. In his mind, he was still #2 to the Nephites. That's right, we were his next target! But Amalickiah knew the Lamanites weren't ready to go to war against us. So after increasing his power and influence among the Lamanites, he then needed to increase the Lamanites' hatred toward the Nephites.

CHAPTER 6
CAPTAIN MORONI'S PREPARATIONS

Amalickiah's propaganda campaign consisted of building towers throughout the Lamanite cities and, at certain hours of the day, every day, paying people to stand on the towers to spread lies about the Nephites. Amalickiah also paid them to tell the Lamanites how awesome he was. It's like he took what the Zoramites had been doing with the Rameumptom, tinkered with it, and added nitro boosters. Amalickiah knew that if the Lamanites heard these lies frequently enough, they would begin to believe them. And so he began to rebuild the wall of hatred around the Lamanites.

I, however, had been building different kinds of walls. Mormon records, "Now it came to pass that while Amalickiah had thus been obtaining power by fraud and deceit, Moroni, on the other hand, had been preparing the minds of the people to be faithful unto the Lord their God."[29] For me, faith has always been an action. If I have faith that the bridge will sustain me, then I show it by stepping out confidently onto the bridge.

I knew armor was not going to be enough this time. Amalickiah, like Zerahemnah before him, had convinced himself that we had only defeated the Lamanites because of our armor. Seriously, that logic just kills me! How do you ignore five hundred years of military triumphs? We hadn't used armor for five hundred years, and

29. Alma 48:7.

now we're only victorious because of armor?! I still feel like it's the daftest thing I've ever heard.

What *was* true is that the Nephites suffered far fewer deaths in the most recent war because of the armor. And, that led me to my next idea . . .

If armor worked for *people*, why not for *cities*? Armor makes it harder for weapons to hurt a person, so why not make it harder for the Lamanite armies to hurt our cities?

So that's what I did, I armored our cities. I actually began our city fortification project right after Amalickiah escaped into the woods. While my idea was met with some support at the time, it is safe to say that support was strengthened significantly once we received reports that Amalickiah had become king of the Lamanites.

Our fortification project was, shall we say, *elaborate*. I knew that occasionally Nephite armies became caught between cities without necessary provisions or a nearby fortified location we could use to retreat or to regroup. To remedy this problem, we built small forts in strategic locations. These forts were walled enclosures, sometimes made from dirt that we had piled and packed high, and sometimes made from stone.

We also enlisted the citizens from each city to work together with our soldiers to build walls around each city. Most of these walls followed the same pattern. First, we dug a deep trench around each city and used the dirt from the trenches to build up a wall behind each trench. This made it so that the wall was twice as high, because the Lamanites would have to descend into the trench before then attempting to climb the

dirt wall formed from the dirt removed to create the trench in the first place.

Next, we sunk posts into the tops of these dirt walls, and then we built a tall fence around the city. Running along the inside of the fence was a wooden walkway that could be used by the Nephites to watch for invading armies, and also to shoot arrows when necessary. At the corners of each fence, we built tall towers that gave even better visibility and provided even better opportunities to shoot arrows and other projectiles.

I knew from past experience that the Lamanites used Nephite dissenters as their chief captains. They did this for at least two different reasons. First, as we have discussed previously, the Nephite dissenters hated the Nephites more than your average, friendly, local Lamanite; and second, the Nephite dissenters were more familiar with our cities, our tactics, our strengths, and our weaknesses.

I began to consider our security from the viewpoint of a dissenter. What would a dissenter tell the Lamanite army about our cities and our army? What knowledge of our infrastructure did Amalickiah carry with him that he could now exploit?

Again, this is me coming up with a plan, not just sitting around hoping the Lord would protect us. The Lord doesn't just give us the answers—He expects us to meet Him in the middle. Remember the brother of Jared? When he needed light in the boats, the Lord didn't just give him the answer. He asked the brother of Jared to come up with a solution and get back to Him. Do you think the Lord didn't have any ideas Himself? I'm pretty sure the Lord was trying to teach us all something when He sent the brother of Jared back to the drawing board.

After some thought, the brother of Jared decided he needed glowing stones. So he made the best stones he could and then brought them back up the mountain to ask God to light them up. I thought about the brother of Jared a lot while I was chief captain. In my mind, each different thing I did to protect my people was like fashioning a stone for the Lord to light up. I decided to make as many stones as I possibly could and pray like crazy that God would touch them and make them light up.

I wasn't praying for God to literally touch the walls I was building and make them glow, but rather for Him to bless each and every one of our efforts to help protect ourselves, no matter how small. Sometimes in your life you will work hard for something that may seem out of reach. In a way, when you pray for God's help in your efforts, it is as if you come before him with your little pile of stones, asking him to justify and magnify your efforts by touching them and lighting them up. Too often we pray for light but don't take the time to create the stones.

So back to me "thinking like a dissenter." Satan does this all the time, but in reverse. He takes good things, like TV, internet, and phones, and figures out how to use them for bad. I, on the other hand, by trying to think like a dissenter, was taking a bad thing—a dissenter who wants to destroy the Nephites—and figuring out how to prevent him from doing bad. I wasn't ignoring potential problems or weaknesses; I was trying to get ahead of them.

Earlier, we talked about making a plan to resist temptation. One of the ways to do this is to look around at friends, family members, or acquaintances who perhaps haven't made the best choices. If you think about their lives and how they might have been able to choose differently in certain key situations, you can prepare yourself to make better choices if you encounter those same circumstances. Nephi certainly learned a lot by watching his older brother Laman's decision making. Perhaps, when confronted with important, difficult decisions, Nephi asked himself, "What would Laman do?" and then worked to do the exact opposite.

Laman's life was corrupted by his bad decision making, so Nephi could avoid negative consequences in his own life by pointedly and thoughtfully learning from Laman's poor choices.

Sometimes, Satan is so effective at corrupting good things that we forget they were good in the first place. Television and the internet are important and powerful tools of communication, tools the Lord helped inspire as a means of sharing the gospel. "Thinking like a dissenter" doesn't mean completely avoiding TV and the internet—it means taking time to think about how to use them effectively for wholesome entertainment, information, and missionary uses. Anything Satan can use for evil, you can probably figure out a way to use for good. I promise it's worth the time and thought to do so. One name for this process is "reverse engineering," or taking something apart to figure out how it works so you can rebuild it for your own righteous purposes.

There are lots of examples of this kind of faithful reverse engineering. For example, think of the holidays. Easter, Halloween, and even Christmas began as pagan holidays that had nothing to do with Christ or goodness. Over time, good people have hijacked these holidays and turned them for good. Easter used to celebrate a false goddess whose symbol was a rabbit, and now it celebrates the resurrection of Christ. Faithful Christians replaced pagan celebrations that used to occur in December with Christmas, turning something worldly into a celebration of the birth of Christ.

As for Halloween, I'm pretty sure you can tell that Halloween was never about Christ, but today its predominant activity is handing out candy to all the neighbor kids. Say what you will about Halloween, but I say handing out candy to neighborhood children is a great example of good people turning something negative into a positive. What I really want to know, however, is why there is no Captain Moroni costume out there! Let's go, people! Someone needs to make that happen!

Seriously, though, if you think about it, the forces of good and evil still fight over these holidays. The world wants us to focus on celebrating the Easter Bunny (not real) and Santa (totally real) instead of Christ's Resurrection and birth. The world would have us knock over garbage cans and engage in general mayhem on Halloween rather than encourage the good children of the earth to dress up as their favorite Nephite chief captain and collect candy door-to-door.

Look, all I'm saying is that if some little kid knocked on my door on Halloween evening in a Captain Moroni costume, I would give him a lot of candy. A *lot*!

This battle between purity and corruption is constant: Satan tries to take good things and convince us to use them for evil, and we try to clean up and purify anything Satan has corrupted. This conflict is important to understand, Buttercup. At all times, we are either cleaning up the world or making it messier. It is our choice. For our purposes in this book, all you need to know is that while the Lamanites were trying to exploit the dissenters' inside information about the Nephites, I was trying to imagine how those conversations were playing out so that we could stay one step ahead of Amalickiah's evil plots.

I'm here to tell you that getting inside the head of a dissenter was illuminating. I realized some of our cities were sitting ducks. These cities were easy pickings for the Lamanites, and taking them over first would give the Lamanites a strong foothold into our land, one that would be difficult to push them out of.

So I focused our efforts on fortifying these weaker cities. I anticipated that the Lamanites would go to these cities first, so I decided I could use that knowledge against them. I wanted the Lamanites to show up at those cities thinking they were going to be able to manhandle us as usual, but instead they would find stronger cities than they had ever seen. A massive disappointment just might completely demoralize the Lamanites.

We strengthened the weakest cities the most, and the rest as best we could. We placed a greater number of soldiers in cities that we were unable to fortify as much as we wanted. In short, we did everything we could possibly do to qualify for God's assistance. Was it enough? Of course not! The Lamanites still outnumbered us by a massive amount, but we knew that it was only "by grace that we are saved, after all we can do."[30] The record says:

> And this was their faith, that by so doing God would prosper them in the land, or in other words, if they were faithful in keeping the commandments of God that he would prosper them in the land; yea, warn them to flee, or to prepare for war, according to their danger;
>
> And also, that God would make it known unto them whither they should go to defend themselves against their enemies, and by so doing, the Lord would deliver them; and this was the faith of Moroni, and his heart did glory in it; not in the shedding of blood but in doing good, in preserving his people, yea, in keeping the commandments of God, yea, and resisting iniquity.[31]

30. 2 Nephi 25:23.
31. Alma 48:15–16.

Four years passed as we prepared for Amalickiah's return. Four long years spent fortifying our cities, our armies, and our faith. We were fashioning as many stones as possible and praying constantly that God would touch them and light them up for us, proverbially speaking. And Mormon recorded that never was there a happier time among the Nephites than during my day. I don't know if he's right: I didn't live during the rest of the time. But I do know that we *were* happy those four years. We were working together, and there were no wars among us. It was a wonderful time.

And we didn't just work hard; we played hard, too. The Book of Mormon doesn't spend much time on Nephite recreation, but we had a lot of fun together. The great thing about being righteous and becoming "one" is that it fosters and highlights each individual's unique personality and ability. That's right, you heard me: righteousness creates uniqueness. When Christ commands us to be one, like He and the Father are one, He is not telling us to have the same personality. Nope. The more Christlike we become, the more we become our own best, unique self. Becoming one means becoming one in purpose, and character. We can all attain the character of Christ, while stim maintaining our own unique character.

Character and personality are very different. Trust me, I'm coming to you after having spent a couple thousand years up in heaven, and I assure you that there are a *lot* of unique personalities up here! Joseph Smith taught that the same sociability that exists on earth exists in heaven, and he's right, but I have to say, people are even funnier in heaven. You should see Elijah when he starts reenacting his challenge with the priests of Baal. Man, that guy has a sense of humor. "Where is your God? Perhaps he is away hunting, or asleep . . . ?"[32] Can you believe Elijah poured that many barrels of water over the wood and stones before it caught on fire? You can definitely add him to your list of people not to mess with: Santa and Elijah.

32. See 1 Kings 18:27.

Anyway, we were happier than we had ever been, but it was short-lived. Soon the Lamanites were preparing for war once more. The record says:

> Notwithstanding their peace amongst themselves, they were compelled reluctantly to contend with their brethren, the Lamanites. . . .
>
> Now, they were sorry to take up arms against the Lamanites, because they did not delight in the shedding of blood; yea, and this was not all—they were sorry to be the means of sending so many of their brethren out of this world into an eternal world, unprepared to meet their God.
>
> Nevertheless, they could not suffer to lay down their lives, that their wives and their children should be massacred by the barbarous cruelty of those who were once their brethren, yea, and had dissented from their church, and had left them and had gone to destroy them by joining the Lamanites.
>
> Yea, they could not bear that their brethren should rejoice over the blood of the Nephites, so long as there were any who should keep the commandments of God, for the promise of the Lord was, if they should keep his commandments they should prosper in the land.[33]

33. Alma 48:21–25.

CAPTAIN'S LOG

- Beware of Satan's propaganda
- Faith is an action
- We can protect our homes with spiritual armor
- Learn from dissenters, stay one step ahead
- The Lord expects us to work to defend ourselves
- Pray for God to light up your righteous efforts
- Ask yourself if your choices are cleaning up the world or making it messier
- Someone should create a Captain Moroni Halloween costume
- Focus on strengthening your weaknesses
- God will warn you of danger through the Spirit
- Righteousness creates uniqueness
- Don't mess with Elijah

CHAPTER 7

AMALICKIAH'S RETURN (KIND OF)

On November 10, during the ninteenth year of the reign of the judges, the Lamanite armies were seen approaching the land of Ammonihah. You may recall that the Lamanites had destroyed Ammonihah once before. In only one day. Suffice it to say, they thought it would be easy pickings, especially since the Lamanites now had armor of their own. I wonder where they came up with *that* idea. Hmm . . .

The Lamanites thought they were going to mop up the earth with us now that they had armor. Amalickiah was so confident, he didn't even come along for the fight. It reminds me a bit of King David not going out to war and getting himself into trouble because of it. For some reason, pride often causes people to shun the fight. Amalickiah was sure the Lamanites would make short work of us, and he stayed behind to plan his triumphant entry into the city of Zarahemla, as king over the whole land. Let's just say that his plans were . . . premature.

When the Lamanite captains saw the fortifications at Ammonihah, they were shocked, just like we planned! We were prepared for them in a manner that never had been known among the children of Lehi. If Amalickiah had been there, he might have just forced his soldiers to attack, because he didn't care about the lives of his people.[34] Cooler heads prevailed among his captains, and the Lamanite army retreated to the wilderness to regroup. The dissenters got together, compared their thoughts on Nephite weaknesses, and said, "Let's attack the city of Noah! That was always one of the weaker cities!"[35]

The chief captains agreed, and they took an oath that they would destroy all the people of the city of Noah.[36] Yeah, not a good idea. We've already talked about how seriously the Lamanites take their oaths, and this one was about to backfire.

When the Lamanites arrived at Noah, they were dumbfounded. The city of Noah was even stronger than the city of Ammonihah! This was by design. I predicted that the Lamanites would first go to Ammonihah and then to Noah, and I specifically made Noah as formidable as possible. And I had a little surprise for the Lamanites. I placed my main man Lehi in charge of the army at the city of Noah. First the Lamanites freaked out when they saw the fortifications of the city. Then they freaked out even more when they found out that Lehi commanded the city!

---

34. Alma 49:10.
35. See Alma 49:12.
36. Alma 49:13.

Let's just say they really, *really* wanted to retreat again. And they probably would have, if not for that teensy weensy little oath their chief captains had made. So they moved toward the city. The only way to get in was through the gated entrance, so that was where Lehi concentrated his forces. The Nephites picked off the Lamanites in droves from their perches above the fence. After suffering an immense slaughter, the Lamanites began trying to dig down the dirt walls. But they were swept off by the stones and arrows that were thrown at them, and instead of filling up the ditches by pulling down the dirt, the ditches began to fill with their dead and wounded bodies.[37]

The Lamanites kept at it until all their chief captains were killed. By then, more than one thousand of the Lamanites had perished—and not a single Nephite. Some of our men had been wounded, but not a single Nephite died in the battle. You heard me right . . . zero Nephite casualties. "Zero" never sounded so awesome.

37. Alma 49:22.

CHAPTER 8

AMALICKIAH'S RASH PROMISE

As soon as the Lamanites noticed all their chief captains were dead, they fled into the wilderness, returned to Amalickiah, and informed him of their massive loss. Amalickiah, who thought he was on the verge of the greatest victory over the Nephites of all time, had just suffered the worst Lamanite loss *ever*: one thousand deaths to none.

After hearing of the magnitude of the loss and realizing the error of his ways, Amalickiah retired to a quiet life of farming.

Yeah, I wish. No, actually, Amalickiah was livid. And for some reason that totally escapes me, he was especially angry with little old me. Can you believe it? All I did was try to protect my people. What's wrong with that? Anyway, he was so mad at me that right then and there he made an oath of his own. Amalickiah swore that he would drink my blood. I didn't even know I was on the menu! Does a cup of my blood come with one of those little paper umbrellas? Gross! Gross! Gross!

Chocolate milk time! Yay! Go and get it! I'll wait right here!

What? You're not thirsty? Why not? I don't understand. You love thick, creamy chocolate milk! Nope? Not right now? Alright, suit yourself.

Anyway, back to Amalickiah wanting to drink my blood. I'm not sure what drinking my blood was going to do for Amalickiah, but that's what he wanted. I thought about sending him some

fancy baked bread with a note that said, "This particular bread really brings out the flavor of my blood. FYI."

My wife didn't think that was nearly as funny as I did, so I didn't go through with it. But I still think it's funny. My son Moronihah did, too. He cracked jokes about my blood at the dinner table for a week before my wife threatened to make him do the dishes for the whole neighborhood if he didn't stop.

Amalickiah's anger led him to do something rash, to make a promise that he would regret. Anger almost always leads to regret. When we are angry, we are selfish, and both faith and spirit diminish. Anger is very fertile ground for temptation. In general, you should not allow yourself to make decisions while angry. Calm yourself down first. This applies to all decisions, including your media choices.

As for me, my blood was safe for the time being. After our massive victory, five peaceful years went by before Amalickiah returned. We continued to strengthen our fortifications during that time, and we built many more cities.

CHAPTER 9

A SEASON OF PEACE

There are a couple of meaningful events from that five year period of peace that we should cover. First is Morianton. The land of Morianton bordered the land of Lehi, both of which were by the seashore. A dispute arose among them. Morianton's people thought a portion of the land belonged to them, and the people of Lehi disagreed. The disagreement escalated until finally the people of Morianton took up their weapons to take the land by force. Rather than fight, the people of Lehi came to me to ask for my help.

A simple review of the property records made it clear that the people of Lehi were not in the wrong, and that Morianton and his people were just making a land grab. Once Morianton heard that I was getting involved, he convinced his people to flee to the north. We already had the Lamanites pinned down to the south, and I did not want another angry, violent group of people populating the north.

The only reason we found out about Morianton's plan is that a maidservant of his fled from him and told us. Apparently, Morianton was a man of much passion, and he became angry with this woman and fell upon her and beat her much.[38]

Now, I know there are both young men and young women reading this right now. (Yes, I can see you, Buttercup!) But for all of you young men, you had better watch yourself. I have never

38. Alma 50:30.

understood how a man could hit a woman or a child. Such behavior is unacceptable. Nephi specifically stated that everyone who reads the words of the Book of Mormon will one day stand before him and know that he and the other prophets of the Book of Mormon were commanded to write the words found therein.[39] Well, Nephi and I have a little deal. Anyone who has hit or harmed a woman or child will also have to stand before *me.* I assure you, I will have just left the gym, my muscles will be rippling, and the "meeting" will not be pleasant.

My notes say I'm supposed to move on now and talk about how Nephihah, the chief judge, passed away and was replaced by Pahoran. However, talking about Morianton and his treatment of women has really ticked me off. It dawns on me that some of you reading this book might wonder why being chaste and pure is so important. To explain, I'm going to use an example used by many Book of Mormon prophets: a tree. There are lots of parables about trees in the Book of Mormon: the tree of life in Lehi's dream, the allegory of the olive tree in Jacob 5, Alma's tree of faith in Alma 28, etc.

For our purposes today, I am going to focus on the allegory of the olive tree in Jacob 5. In that parable, the master and his servant tried so very hard to preserve those olive trees. Notwithstanding their efforts, the trees continued to die. At one point, the servant shared a hypothesis with the master, a reason why he suspected the trees may be dying. Jacob 5:48 says, "And it came to pass that the servant said unto his master: Is it not the loftiness of thy vineyard—have not the branches thereof overcome the roots which are good? And because the branches have overcome the roots thereof, behold they grew faster than the strength of the roots, taking strength unto themselves. Behold, I say, is not this the cause that the trees of thy vineyard have become corrupted?"

I want you to imagine that you begin dating someone. Once you start dating, your relationship is like a small potted tree. Like the tree, your relationship is young and small. As you continue to

39. 2 Nephi 33:11.

date, and as you show sincere concern and appreciation for one another, the tree begins to slowly grow. The pot is symbolic. Before marriage, a relationship can only grow so much. You aren't spending all your time together, you haven't made eternal commitments to each other or covenants with God regarding your relationship. The pot limits the growth of the relationship until marriage. The tree trunk can only get so big, and only so many branches can grow. Then one day, if you decide to marry, together you lift the tree out of the pot and plant it carefully in temple soil, allowing for significantly greater growth all around.

Now, let's back up and zoom in on that small potted tree for a moment. The roots signify the healthy aspects of your relationship, things you appreciate about each other, the mutual respect you are building together, and kindness and service you show one another. The branches and leaves symbolize something as well. Every time you hold hands, a small green leaf unfolds. Every hug, every gentle brush of the arm is another leaf. These things are exciting and can be wonderful between kind and clean young men and young women who are committed to the Lord.

However, sometimes the tree can get twiggy and overgrown when the leaves began to multiply too early, too quickly, or too far. This happens when the physical aspect becomes the focus of the relationship for one or both of the individuals. Remember, this tree is still in its pot. The roots can only grow so wide and so deep while still in the pot. It takes a lot of strength from the roots to create leaves and branches. Like the olive trees in Jacob 5, if the leaves and branches of your relationships start to take strength unto themselves, it creates a dangerous situation for a young potted tree. The roots start winding around in the pot, and nutrients become scarcer and scarcer. When the focus of the relationship, for one or for both of you, becomes the leaves and not the roots, the tree will die.

Imagine once again that day in the temple, kneeling across the altar from your eternal companion. He or she will be the one you'll spend the rest of your life with, and beyond. Imagine that person looking at you and asking, "How many dead trees are in your forest?" What will your response be? Remember, every relationship doesn't have to end as a dead tree. Sometimes you or the person you are dating will just decide that the relationship isn't supposed to continue, that together you are not the best fit. This happens all the time, and it can end on healthy, friendly terms. It is one thing to take the tree back to the tree nursery still very much alive, and another thing to kill the tree.

If possible, you should date many people before marriage. You should get to know as many people as possible. Dating a variety of people will teach you about yourself, about being a kind and thoughtful person, and about the attributes you want in your eternal companion. Only one of your relationships will end in marriage, but that does not mean that the rest have to become dead trees.

Looking at inappropriate pictures, movies, or TV shows is also not okay. It is using other people for selfish reasons. Viewing inappropriate pictures is not even a real tree; it is like an old neon-orange Christmas tree that's sharp with metal needles and showy, short-circuiting lights. Get too close and all you get are cuts, burns, and blindness.

My young friends, do not be like the Jaredites. Do you remember what we Nephites named the land of the Jaredites? We called it the land of desolation. So great was the destruction the Jaredites wrought upon themselves and the land around them, that no one went in to inhabit the land for many, many years. It was as if there had been an enormous forest fire. The Jaredites gave in to selfishness and violence, and they were all destroyed. The prophet Ether invited them to repent, promising that they would be saved if they would do so. They would not.

Will you repent? Some of you may already have the cuts and burns of the fake neon tree on your hands. Satan will try to tell you that it is too late, that you are too far gone. I assure you that he is wrong! Satan was a liar from the beginning. You are not too far gone, and there are many around you willing to step up and be the Teancums, the Lehis, the Helamans, and the Pahorans in your life.

You see, I didn't defeat Amalickiah on my own, and I didn't defeat him by accident. I had help, we had a plan, and Christ was at the center of that plan. The plan was to work and prepare and prevent as if our lives depended only upon ourselves, and to pray and fast and live as if our safety depended only upon the Lord. And, as you will see, our plan worked.

Now, back to the other significant event that happened during those five years of peace between the two Amalickiah wars. You see, Pahoran became the third chief judge among the Nephites. You may recall that Alma the Younger was the first chief judge. His father, Alma the Elder, had been a high priest under wicked King Noah before repenting. When Alma the Elder got back to Zarahemla, he and King Mosiah became great friends. Based on their conversations, their experiences with their own children, and the inspiration of God, King Mosiah decided not to pass the kingdom to one of his sons, but rather to create an elected position instead.

The recently repentant Alma the Younger became that first elected chief judge. He is a great example of how it is never too late to repent. Alma the Younger had not just made bad choices—he had fought against the Church and tried to convince people not to believe in it! I'm pretty sure you've never done anything like that. If it wasn't too late for Alma the Younger, it isn't too late for you. Believe me!

So after eight years as the first Nephite chief judge, Alma the Younger decided the best way to help people keep the law was to help them to better follow Christ. He stepped down from the judgeship and dedicated himself to preaching the gospel. Alma was replaced by a great man named Nephihah. Shortly after our first defeat of Amalickiah's army, Nephihah passed away. His son was elected to replace him as chief judge, and his name was Pahoran.

I know this seems like some random political information, but I'm telling you this because leadership transitions can be ripe for sowing discord. Amalickiah knew this. Remember, he had first taken advantage of a leadership transition when Helaman replaced Alma as the prophet. That was when he first tried to become king of the Nephites. Now, having learned from his spies that Pahoran was elected as the new chief judge, Amalickiah pounced. Amalickiah still knew a lot of people among the Nephites, powerful people, and he began corresponding secretly with these people. Unfortunately, he found many willing pen pals.

No one ever said Amalickiah was dumb. Scum of the earth, loser of the universe, residue of the toe sweat on my sandal: yes. Dumb: no. Amalickiah realized that one of our biggest strengths as Nephites was our unity. You and I know that the source of our strength was our unity in keeping the commandments of God, which made us worthy of God's blessings and protection. Amalickiah just chalked it up to our loyalty to each other. He decided that if he could disrupt that unity from within, he just might have a chance of defeating us. Even though he didn't fully understand or believe in the source of the power behind our unity, he was still right: our division could lead to our subtraction, and therefore to Amalickiah's multiplication. Whew! That's a lot of math, Buttercup. I need a moment to catch my breath!

CHAPTER 10

AMALICKIAH'S NEW PLAN

Shortly after the election of Pahoran, a group of Amalickiah sympathizers began agitating for change among the Nephites. They were careful, however, and claimed that they just wanted a few particular points of the law to be . . . well, altered. To "alter" something typically means to make small changes to it. You know, like when your biceps get too big for your shirt and you need to add another four inches to the sleeve width? Happens to me all the time.

So when the group asked for "alterations" to the law, we all assumed they meant small changes. As you know, I was open to new ideas, and so were the chief judge, Pahoran, and the prophet, Helaman. The three of us invited the leaders of the agitators to come meet with us to discuss their desired alterations.

After everyone had exchanged pleasantries, Pahoran said, "You have said that you desire a few alterations of the law. What would you have us do?"

The spokesman for the group cleared his throat, smiled, and said, "We are desirous that the law should be altered in a manner to overthrow the free government and to establish a king over the land."[40]

Pin drop.

Let me tell you, Pahoran has ice in his veins, because he didn't even flinch. After a short pause, he cheerfully replied, "Alright, thank you for letting us know your concerns! We will put this request before the people and allow them to vote on it."

40. Alma 51:5.

I was pretty surprised Pahoran was so quick to put this to a vote. But he knew what he was doing. Back when King Mosiah ended the kingship, he said, "It is common for the lesser part of the people to desire that which is not right; therefore this shall ye observe and make it your law—to do your business by the voice of the people."[41] Sure enough, King Mosiah was right. The king-men, as they came to be known, were outvoted by the freemen. Chief Judge Pahoran kept his seat, and surprisingly, the king-men backed down and did not try to enforce their desires with the sword.

The record states that "those who were in favor of kings were those of high birth, and they sought to be kings; and they were supported by those who sought power and authority over the people."[42]

Unfortunately, the king-men's greatest supporter was Amalickiah. The timing of the king-men's protests was not coincidental. "For behold, Amalickiah had again stirred up the hearts of the people of the Lamanites against the people of the Nephites, and he was gathering together soldiers from all parts of his land, and arming them, and preparing for war with all diligence; for he had sworn to drink the blood of Moroni."[43]

Again with the drinking of my blood! What is the deal with Amalickiah and my blood?

I love how Mormon refers to Amalickiah's promise, saying, "But behold, we shall see that his promise which he made was rash."[44] That is some mighty fine writing, Mormon, I have to say—even if it is a bit of a spoiler.

Amalickiah was once again preparing his soldiers for battle, just as we were having a vote

41. Mosiah 29:26.
42. Alma 51:8.
43. Alma 51:9.
44. Alma 51:10.

on whether to have a king. I wish I could say this was a coincidence, but it was not. Nor was it humility that caused the king-men to stand down after the election. They were just biding their time. Once Amalickiah and his armies entered our land, all the king-men refused to fight.

The earlier vote had allowed the king-men to marshall their supporters and garner additional favor. Once the war began, the king-men were mobilized against the freemen. In fact, "When the men who were called king-men had heard that the Lamanites were coming down to battle . . . they were glad in their hearts; and they refused to take up arms, for they were so wroth with the chief judge, and also with the people of liberty, that they would not take up arms to defend their country."[45]

Well, I had a hunch that these king-men were, in fact, colluding with Amalickiah, so I asked Pahoran to hold another vote. This time, the vote was on whether those who refused to go and fight Amalickiah could be considered in league with Amalickiah and therefore enemies to the Nephites, punishable by death. The people voted to grant the government this authority, and my armies marched forth against the king-men, destroying any who would not take up arms for their country.

I could not believe that after all that had happened, and all the destruction that Amalickiah had wrought, he was able to infiltrate

45. Alma 51:13.

so far among the Nephites. In the past, dissenters had always just left and gone straight to the Lamanites. I have to admit that from a military perspective, Amalickiah's idea to create dissension, and then encourage the dissenters to stay among the Nephites to weaken the nation, was a brilliant tactical move. This is something you should watch out for in your day, and another reason it is so important to listen to the modern prophets and apostles.

While we were focused on the king-men, Amalickiah was already in our borders, taking city after city. We were spread too thin. By the time we handled the dissenters, Amalickiah's army was entrenched in many of our own cities and were using our own fortifications against us. With their numberless hosts and the use of our own fortified cities, the Lamanites then mounted an offensive against Bountiful—our temple city.

But Amalickiah's efforts to take Bountiful were rebuffed by Teancum and his men, "for they were great warriors; for every man of Teancum did exceed the Lamanites in their strength and in their skill of war, insomuch that they did gain advantage over the Lamanites."[46]

Teancum and his men harassed the Lamanites all day and into the evening. Finally, Teancum caused that his men should set up camp in the borders of Bountiful, near the seashore. Amalickiah's men set camp nearby, on the beach itself.

46. Alma 51:31.

CHAPTER 11

AMALICKIAH HAS TO DIE-AH

Everyone was worn out by the labors and heat of the day. But Teancum couldn't sleep. He kept thinking there must be something more he could do. Finally, he decided to take matters into his own hands. He grabbed his most trusted assistant, and together they snuck into the camp of Amalickiah in the middle of the night. The Lamanites were so tired, even their guards had fallen asleep. But how to find the tent of Amalickiah? Fortunately for Teancum, it wasn't too hard. One of the tents was not like the others. Apparently Amalickiah liked to sleep in style. Teancum very quietly snuck into the fanciest tent in camp, took his javelin, and stabbed Amalickiah in the heart.

Amalickiah died so quickly, he didn't make a sound. Teancum and his assistant were able to sneak out of camp undetected.

I sometimes wonder what it must have been like for Amalickiah to go to sleep one night and then suddenly wake up in the spirit world. I don't imagine it was a smooth transition for him. Nor do I imagine many mourned his passing. Such a waste of a life. Imagine the good Amalickiah could have done, if only he had *wanted* to do good.

But enough about Amalickiah. Let's talk about Teancum. What an amazing, heroic thing he did! Teancum was up late with an Amalickiah problem, and he didn't give in like Lehonti. Instead, Teancum decided that enough was enough and that he was going to do everything he could to stop Amalickiah. But he didn't go alone. He took a trusted associate with him.

If you think about it, what Teancum did is kind of like going to your knees in prayer if you are struggling with temptation. Teancum did not want a long battle with Amalickiah, and he did not want to fight him alone. Do you want a long battle with temptation? Of course not! Do you think you can defeat serious sin alone? It's harder than you think. The best and first step is being humble enough to kneel down and talk it over with your Heavenly Father. He already knows your thoughts and concerns, so you might as well be honest with Him and seek His help.

Killing Amalickiah didn't automatically end the war with the Lamanites any more than prayer automatically ends the battle with temptation, but it's a great place to start.

Of course, we Nephites hoped that Amalickiah's death *would* mean the end of the war. Unfortunately, our hopes were dashed. Sudden bursts of bravery are nice, but it takes sustained faithful action to defeat opponents like the Lamanites and temptation.

When the Lamanites woke up to find Amalickiah dead, they abandoned their plan to attack Bountiful and quickly retreated to the fortified cities they had already taken. Once there, they

decided on a new leader: Ammoron, Amalickiah's brother. The first thing Ammoron did was return to the Lamanite capital city to let the queen know of Amalickiah's death. While he was there, he recruited reinforcements and came up with a new plan.

Ammoron's plan was to divide his army and open up a new battlefront. The Lamanite army had already taken many cities on the eastern portion of our land, and now Ammoron decided to send a large army to work on the western side. Thus we were being harassed both on the eastern and western borders of our land. Suffice it to say we found ourselves in very dangerous circumstances.

You know what wasn't in dangerous circumstances anymore? My blood. Well, sure, all the Lamanites still wanted to kill me, but at least my blood was no longer on the menu! My wife was pretty thankful for that. Small victories, right?

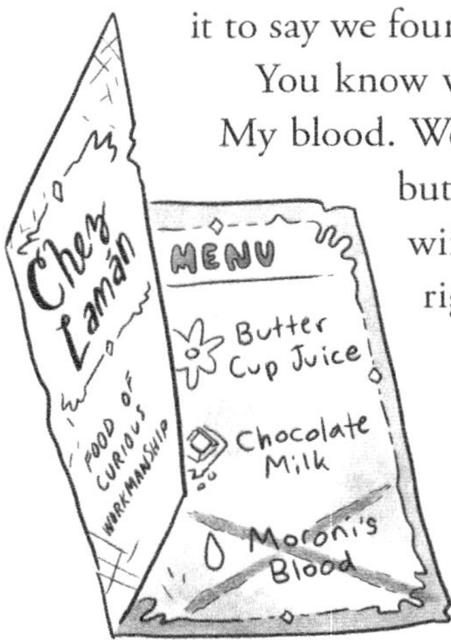

We had several small victories over this time period, including tricking the Lamanites out of their largest stronghold, the city of Mulek. That victory resulted in a lot of Lamanite prisoners. We marched them off to the city of Bountiful, and because it was easier to guard them while they were working, we made them strengthen the city's fortifications. This is actually a useful idea for combating temptation. Make your weaknesses work for you! You can use this for any kind of temptation. Anytime there is something that is tempting you, you can plan to do something specific whenever that temptation arises. For example, if you are struggling with unclean thoughts, you can plan to sing a hymn, or read your scriptures, or practice memorizing "The Family: A Proclamation to the World." By replacing negative thoughts with uplifting, clean actions, over time you fortify yourself against temptation, just like our Lamanite prisoners helped fortify our own cities.

An important part of using your weaknesses to become strong is being honest with yourself. You have to admit to yourself that a particular temptation is lingering more than it should before you can make an effective plan to overcome it. As long as you pretend you're fine, you'll never make a plan. Coming up with a plan to use temptation as a reminder to do positive and worthwhile things will help you convert temptation into goodness. At the end of the day, it is goodness that we should all strive for. Checking off boxes is not the point; it is just a means to the end goal of righteousness.

Something that really helps me to plan for goodness is the doctrine of the three degrees of glory. Joseph Smith's revelation about the three degrees of glory is one of the most important revelations of the Restoration. You may recall the names of the three degrees of glory: the telestial, terrestrial, and celestial kingdoms. Until this revelation, the Christian world just believed in heaven and hell. The idea of only heaven or hell is actually one of the greatest tricks of Satan. If there are only two places to go after life, heaven or hell, there is no real reason to develop goodness. Logically, if I don't do anything *too* too bad, I'm not going to go to hell, and so by default, I go to heaven. Heaven is the only other option.

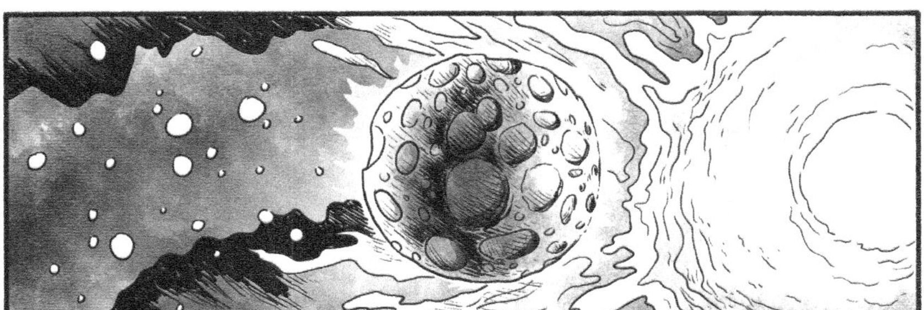

This is a terrible way to live—trying not to do anything *too* bad. If there is only heaven and hell, there is no incentive to develop Christlike goodness. The fact is, people who are trying not to do anything too bad are really just living a telestial life.

Sometimes people living a telestial life consider doing something good and then decide not to do it because their heart is not really into it. They think acting insincerely is worse than not acting at all. Unfortunately, they are missing something important. Those people are expecting to make a leap from telestial living to celestial living all at once, meaning they think one day they'll just suddenly have a desire to do the right things for the right reasons with no effort on their part. But that's not possible.

If we don't have a testimony of something—like fasting, for example—we don't need to wait for a testimony to come before fasting. The testimony of fasting comes *from* fasting! The key is not to just go hungry for a couple of meals because we are supposed to fast, but to fast with faith: "Heavenly Father, people say this fasting thing is very important. Right now, I don't get it. However, I have felt the Spirit in other areas of my life, and I would like to know if fasting is really a commandment and will really bless the lives of those I fast for. I am going to fast even though I don't understand, but please bless me as I do so, that I may gain a testimony of the power of fasting."

Together, that prayer and an effort to fast equals terrestrial living! That person is willing to move out of the telestial world and pass through the terrestrial world on their way to a celestial life. A prayer of faith combined with fasting opens the door for the Spirit to confirm the power of fasting in your life. Once you receive that confirmation from God, you then begin fasting at a celestial level. We actually can't live a celestial life on our own; it is the Lord who gets us there. When a person is willing to live terrestrially by living any commandment with a prayer of faith, the Spirit will eventually powerfully confirm the truthfulness and blessings of that commandment, and a testimony is born! Joyfully living the commandments with a testimony of their truthfulness is celestial living.

This framework applies to every facet of the gospel. Like Alma's tree in Alma 28, when you test the gospel by living it with faith, you learn that it is true. But you should not cast aside your faith, because there is more to learn. That original testimony is like a small uncut diamond. Each time we gain a testimony of a different aspect of the gospel, it is as if a new facet is cut on the diamond. It is the facets of a diamond that catch and reflect light. Incidentally, diamonds are cut with diamond saws, diamond dust, and olive oil. The diamond dust and olive oil are mixed together on a cutting wheel called a scaife to cut and polish diamonds. The diamond dust and olive oil are like Christ and His Atonement. Christ's testimony is perfect just as Christ Himself is perfect. He has perfect knowledge and faith, and He suffered for us in the Garden of Gethsemane, an olive tree garden.

When we live with faith, He cuts the facets of our testimony with His own testimony and sacrifice. And the more facets we have to our testimony, the more of the light of Christ we can receive and reflect. He is the light, not us. Over time, and with effort and Christ's help, our testimonies can grow brighter and brighter until the perfect day.

We can also apply this process to defeating sin and temptation. The Church is full of people who have learned to overcome temptations that afflicted them earlier in their lives. For example, Alma, Ammon, Amulek, Zeezrom, and Corianton each rebelled against God when they were younger, but then repented and became amazing missionaries! In the New Testament, Saul fought against the Christians and sought to have them imprisoned. He too repented, and he became Paul, a legendary missionary.

In your day, many who once struggled with looking at inappropriate images have come to see other people as the children of God that they are, and they are unwilling to treat anyone as an object. They have learned to love others too much to use their body, or pictures of their body, for selfish purposes. Using people for any reason is *telestial* living; seeking to bless all people because we are filled with the love of God for His children is *celestial* living. In order to live a celestial life (which is very doable) you first need to be willing to live terrestrially. You need to be willing to combine prayers of faith with a plan for goodness and stick to that plan. Over time, true goodness will come, line upon line and precept upon precept. Like I said earlier, the first step is to be honest with yourself and accept that you have weaknesses, and the next is to come up with a plan.

It's time for me to be honest with myself as well. Even though we experienced some small victories during the period of the war after Ammoron took over, we were in trouble. We had lost many, many cities, and we were practically surrounded. Fighting a two-front war against a much larger army was slowly draining our nation. We needed help.

Well, help came from a very unexpected source. Remember the people of Ammon? When the people of Ammon (who had been Lamanites) were converted, they covenanted never again to take up their weapons of war. But when they saw the difficulty we were having with the Lamanites, many of them believed that the time had come to join the Nephite armies. Many of the Ammonites felt that God had accepted their offering but that He would understand that the Nephites needed help and that survival was more important than their covenant not to fight.

I need help now too—help telling this story. I couldn't defeat the Lamanites on my own, and I can't help you overcome temptation in all of its varieties on my own either. So I am bringing in reinforcements. There is no one better able to tell you about the army of Helaman than Helaman himself. I love the stripling warriors. I also love that I have absolutely nothing to do with the stripling warriors. I was on the other side of the country from them. I was not their captain, and I did not convince them to join the army. You know, I lured you into reading this book with my name and my story, but I hope you can see the truth now: This is not *my* story. This is *our* story. This is me, Teancum, Lehi, Helaman, Pahoran, and all the faithful Nephites we served with working together to obtain the Lord's help to defeat the Lamanites. This was a group effort. We couldn't succeed alone, and neither will you.

So here he is, son of Alma the Younger, grandson of Alma the Elder, prophet extraordinaire, and leader of the stripling warriors! Without further ado, I give you Helaman!

- Do the right thing fast, like Teancum
- Make your weaknesses work for you
- Replace bad thoughts with good works
- Be honest with yourself about your weaknesses
- We must live terrestrially before we can live celestially
- A testimony is like a diamond
- People are children of God, not objects

CHAPTER 12

HELAMAN'S WARRIORS

HELAMAN: Thank you, Moroni. I appreciate the kind introduction! You know, I've been listening to you, and before you take a well-deserved break, there is something very important that I feel like I need to clarify for our young friends: I have, with my own eyes, seen Captain Moroni with a man bun!

MORONI: Whoa! Helaman, I was very, *very* young! It was just a phase! You can't hold that against a guy!

HELAMAN: Look, just because you no longer think man buns are cool does not mean that you always felt that way. People, this guy was proud of his man bun! If you would have asked him then, he would have told you he *invented* the man bun!

MORONI: Alright, Helaman, I'm beginning to think it was a mistake bringing you here! And, to clarify, what I used to say was, "I didn't invent the man bun, but I'm the first guy who made it look good!" There, are you happy now? Can we get back to Amalickiah and the stripling warriors? Huh?

HELAMAN: Alright, alright! I'll give it a rest, but I can't say the same for the other Moroni, Mormon's son—you know, the one on the temples? He asked me to remind you he's pretty muscular himself, and that you are *terrible* on the trombone.

MORONI: Sheesh, everyone's a critic! I'm going to go get something to eat, and it is *not* going to be a green smoothie. They're all yours, Helaman! *(Moroni leaves.)*

HELAMAN: Hey, everybody, it's nice to be here! I love Captain Moroni, and, I have to admit, he did look pretty good with a man bun. I was a little jealous, and I like to give him a hard time. By the way, when a man has a ponytail, why isn't it called a stallion-tail instead of a ponytail? I'm super jazzed to talk to you about the stripling warriors! When I heard that the people of Ammon wanted to join the war, I immediately went out to the land of Jershon to meet with them and to discuss their concerns. I agreed with their point that our armies needed help. I also believed that the Ammonites were sincere in their desire to help and that their hearts were very much in the right place. Nevertheless, I did not feel right about them joining the war.

You see, Ammon and my father were great friends, and Ammon spent a lot of time with my family when I was growing up. I remembered Ammon's stories about his mission among the Lamanites. I remembered Ammon talking about when these Lamanite converts had buried their weapons of war, and the sacred way he described how those men went out to meet the Lamanite army, only to kneel down and begin to pray. Over a thousand Ammonites were killed while on their knees in prayer.

So when I went to Jershon, I shared Ammon's story in his words with the people of Ammon, and I testified of the sacrifice of those thousand men and of how their refusal to fight led to the conversion of more than a thousand Lamanites. Of course, the people also all remembered these stories—they had lived them. But hearing my words and feeling the spirit of my testimony and my love for Ammon, they were convinced that it was not God's will that they break their covenant of peace. That covenant was too important, too precious.

It was in a moment of silence after this outpouring of the Spirit, when hearts were tender and faith was strong, that one young man stood up. He said, "Forgive me for speaking, and for intruding on the sacredness of the spirit we all feel here this day. I, too, feel that the covenant should be kept. I have heard these stories from my earliest recollection. These events are a part of us, a part of me. Nevertheless, it has occurred to me during this meeting—and powerfully so—that *I* was not a part of that covenant. I was too young to make those promises, and as I was just a child, I was not guilty of the sins that motivated them in the first place. I do not mean to contradict what has been decided today. I only want to point out that there are those among us, young men like myself, who were too young to have entered into the covenant of peace, but who are now old enough to join the war." After a short pause, he continued, "Can't *we* help?"[47]

The room fell silent. The young man was right, of course, but there was no joy in his correctness. The righteous never rejoice in war, but rather resign themselves to it. And so it was that the army of Helaman was created. It turned out that at that time there were exactly

47. See Alma 53:10–18.

two thousand young men who were too young to have entered into the covenant of peace but who were now old enough to join the army. They asked me to be their leader—it was a bittersweet honor.

The stripling warriors are a good example of the either/or dilemma. Sometimes we convince ourselves that certain situations have to be *either* one thing *or* another. The stripling warriors showed that it was possible for the people of Ammon to keep their promise *and* to help the war effort. Satan often takes advantage of the either/or dilemma. For example, he may try to convince us that if we go meet with the bishop to discuss repentance it will be too painful. Either we continue in sin and aren't embarrassed, or we go in to talk to the bishop and are embarrassed forever. This is a lie. In fact, going in to see the bishop means the sweet beginning of repentance and the beginning of the end of enslavement to serious sin. It means freedom.

Don't get caught in the either/or trap. Instead, be like the stripling warriors, for "they were exceedingly valiant for courage, and also for strength and activity; but behold, this was not all—they were men who were true at all times in whatsoever thing they were entrusted. Yea, they were men of truth and soberness, for they had been taught to keep the commandments of God and to walk uprightly before him."[48]

Once the stripling warriors were trained and outfitted, I led them to the battlefront and we joined the army of Antipus, another great Nephite warrior. The army of Antipus was stationed near the city Antiparah, a Nephite city that had been taken by one of the largest Lamanite armies. Antipus was charged with defeating that army and retaking the city. None of his efforts were successful, but after the two thousand stripling warriors arrived, the Lamanites became concerned with our growing forces. Antipus came up with a plan whereby the stripling warriors and I would pass by the city of Antiparah as if to carry provisions to another city. Antipus believed our small, young battalion would be too tempting a conquest for

48. Alma 53:20–21.

the Lamanites to pass up. He was right.

As soon as the stripling warriors passed by the city, the entire Lamanite army in Antiparah took off after us. Then the rest of Antipus's army took off after the Lamanites. The Lamanites were none too happy about this turn of events—they'd fallen right into a trap. While on the move, the Lamanite captains decided the best thing they could do was to catch the stripling warriors first and dispose of us quickly before having to face Captain Antipus's more seasoned warriors.

So the Lamanites picked up their pace, tearing after us. Obviously, we picked up our pace as well. The army of Antipus, realizing what was happening and the peril my little army was in, marched as fast as they possibly could after the Lamanites. The three armies marched at full speed, their lives depending upon it, far into the night. Finally, we all three made camp, seeking some much-needed rest.

In the morning, we awoke to find the Lamanites almost upon us! My stripling warriors quickly broke camp and continued their march. There was something different about this march. As we marched away from the Lamanites, we didn't turn to the left or to the right. By marching straight ahead in an undeviating course away from the Lamanites, we made it more difficult for the Lamanites to catch my young warriors. What things

cause you to turn to the left or to the right in your life? What things slow you down in your eternal progression and make it easier for the adversary to catch up to you?

The Lamanites didn't catch up to us: in fact, we looked back at one point and realized we had not seen any sign of the Lamanites for quite a while. We halted our march and held a council. There were only two options: either the army of Antipus had caught up to the Lamanites and they were right then engaged in battle, or the Lamanite army was attempting to trick us into coming back to them without reinforcements. If Antipus had caught the Lamanites, I knew there was little chance Antipus could win without help. If the Lamanites were lying in wait for us, there was little chance my stripling warriors would survive. Any of them.

So I looked at my sons—for I felt as if I were a father to them all—and asked, "What say ye, my sons, will ye go against them to battle?"[49] The same young man who spoke at the council in Jershon looked at me and said, "Father, we will go and do."

"Like Nephi?" I said.

"Yes, the Lord has blessed us like Nephi," he responded.

"What do you mean, the *Lord* has blessed you?" I asked.

"Our mothers taught us that Nephi was also not happy to leave Jerusalem in the beginning. The difference between Nephi and his older brothers was that Nephi prayed to the Lord to know if his father was truly following God's will. Nephi said that because he prayed, the Lord did visit him and did soften his heart, and because of that, he did not rebel like unto his brothers."[50]

He continued, "What kind of heart needs to be softened, Father?"

"A hard one," I said, beginning to understand.

"Yes, a hard one. Nephi did not pretend to be more than he was. He admitted that he had a hard heart—one that the Lord needed to soften. Why did the Lord soften Nephi's heart?" he asked me.

"Because he prayed," I responded.

---

49. Alma 56:44.
50. See 1 Nephi 2:16.

"Yes, and we have prayed, too. Our mothers taught us that we could be like Nephi. We would not always *feel* like doing what is right, but if we would pray, the Lord would soften our hearts as well. Our hearts are soft, Father. We are ready to go and do like Nephi, not knowing beforehand where we should go or what we should do. We believe the Lord has prepared the way before us," he finished.

"Your mothers are very wise, my son. Your words remind me that in the record, after listening to Nephi say he will go and do what the Lord commands him, 'Lehi was exceedingly happy, for he knew his son had been blessed of the Lord.'[51] Lehi also understood his son Nephi's heart had been softened, and that he had been blessed of the Lord with the 'go and do' attitude. I had not previously made this connection. Thank you for sharing it with me," I finished.

My dear modern-day friends and Saints, "never had I seen so great courage, nay, not amongst all the Nephites. For as I had ever called them my sons (for they were all of them very young) even so they said unto me: Father, behold our God is with us, and he will not suffer that we should fall; then let us go forth; we would not slay our brethren if they would let us alone; therefore let us go, lest they should overpower the army of Antipus. Now they never had fought, yet they did not fear death; and they did think more upon the liberty of their fathers than they did upon their lives; yea, they had been taught by their mothers, that if they did not doubt, God would deliver them. And they rehearsed unto me the words of their mothers, saying: We do not doubt our mothers knew it."[52]

I admit that at first I was confused by the stripling warriors' frequent mention of the faith of their mothers. I wondered why they did not mention their fathers as well. I also wondered at

51. 1 Nephi 3:8.
52. Alma 56:45–48.

how they referred to me not as "captain" but as "father." It was with no small amount of embarrassment I realized that for many of these two thousand stripling warriors, mothers were all they had. I don't know exactly how many of their fathers were among the one thousand killed while on their knees praying before the Lamanite army many years earlier, but it became clear that it was a high percentage. Perhaps they called me "father" because, for many of them, I was the closest thing to a father they had ever known.

Can you imagine the faith of their mothers? Willingly sending their sons out to war after having already lost their husbands years earlier? This is the faith the stripling warriors were referring to when they said, "We do not doubt our mothers knew it." Knew what? The love and power of God, that's what their mothers knew. They knew it and they lived worthy of it. Those stripling warriors were surrounded by the loving protection of God, first because of their faith, second because of the faith of their fathers, who had given their lives to protect a covenant of peace, and third because of the faith of their mothers, who had given their lives in living the commandments.

And so my two thousand stripling warriors and I marched with power back toward the Lamanites. Once again, we did not turn to the left or to the right, but we marched straight toward the fray. When we arrived, we found a terrible battle had commenced. Antipus had been killed, and his army was about to give way before the Lamanites. And they would have, too, if not for my band of

warriors. The Lamanites were pursuing the fleeing army of Antipus when we caught up to them and began to slay them. So great was the force of our attack that the entire Lamanite army turned upon my warriors. When the army of Antipus saw what was happening, they returned to the battle as a group, thus surrounding the Lamanites. This had been the plan all along, and now it was in full force.

The Lamanites began to fall very quickly, and realizing they were surrounded, they soon surrendered. There were thousands of them. As soon as possible following the surrender, I commanded my army to line up so I could count them. To equal parts joy and surprise, I discovered not one stripling warrior had been killed!

The army of Antipus was astounded. They had lost their leader and many of their men. To not have lost a single stripling warrior was truly a miracle. The miracles continued as my young warriors continued to have success in their battles. With that success, however, came a new problem: a massive and growing number of Lamanite prisoners. For some reason, the flow of provisions from Zarahemla had stopped, and we didn't even have sufficient food for ourselves, let alone for the Lamanite prisoners. We received only a small store of provisions and sixty more young warriors from the people of Ammon. The situation became critical, and we decided to send some of the prisoners back to Zarahemla with a part of our army as guards.

Only one day after that contingent left, they returned—without the prisoners. Apparently, Ammoron had sent massive reinforcements of soldiers and provisions, and our company of guards and the prisoners had run right into them! The Lamanite prisoners broke free and joined those reinforcements, and now all of them were on their way back to fight us.

An enormous battle commenced, "and as the remainder of our army were about to give way before the Lamanites, behold, those two thousand and sixty were firm and undaunted. Yea, and they did obey and observe to perform every word of command with exactness; yea, and even according to their faith it was done unto them;

and I did remember the words which they said unto me that their mothers had taught them.[53]

The stripling warriors stayed strong, and the Lamanite army eventually fled, but there were great losses of life on both sides. Immediately after the Lamanites departed, I gave orders that our wounded should be taken from among the dead, and their injuries cared for.

"And it came to pass that there were two hundred, out of my two thousand and sixty, who had fainted because of the loss of blood; nevertheless, according to the goodness of God, and to our great astonishment, and also the joy of our whole army, there was not one soul of them who did perish; yea, and neither was there one soul among them who had not received many wounds."[54]

Every single stripling warrior received many wounds, but not a single one died. Like Moroni said earlier, "zero" had never sounded so good! Considering that a thousand other Nephites were killed in this battle, the stripling warriors' survival was truly astonishing. The other leaders and I did "justly ascribe it to the miraculous power of God, because of the stripling warriors' exceeding faith in that which they had been taught to believe—that there was a just God, and whosoever did not doubt, that they should be preserved by his

53. Alma 57:20–21.
54. Alma 57:25.

marvelous power. Now this was the faith of these of whom I have spoken; they are young, and their minds are firm, and they do put their trust in God continually."[55]

The stripling warriors defeated the Lamanites because the stripling warriors were exactly obedient to my commands. They learned this obedience, and the benefits of being obedient, by listening to and obeying their mothers. Obedience to parents prepares us for obedience to God. I mentioned that the minds of my warriors were firm. What do you think it means to have a firm mind? I believe it means you don't easily give in to temptation or to what others think about you. God wants us to have soft hearts and firm minds. Too often, we are hard-hearted and soft-minded. When our hearts are soft, we are teachable and we are kind to others. When our minds are firm, we do not give in to peer pressure or give up on our goals to improve through keeping the commandments.

Firm minds and soft hearts—this is the exact opposite

55. Alma 57:26–27.

of what Amalickiah wanted. Remember, Amalickiah caused that people should stand on towers and yell lies about the Nephites. Mormon noted that by so doing, Amalickiah did harden their hearts and blind their minds.[56] This is exactly what sin does. It makes us insensitive to other people because it heightens our sensitivities to ourselves and our own desires, to the exclusion of everyone and everything else. Also, sin blinds our minds because it creates unreal and unclean expectations. It trains the mind to see people as objects, not as children of God. If we continue in our sins, our ability to see truth, beauty, and goodness fades until eventually we become blind to them completely.

56. Alma 48:3.

CHAPTER 13

SUCCESS AMIDST SUFFERING

HELAMAN: Like I said, I loved my adopted sons, my stripling warriors. There wasn't anything special about them physically, and they certainly weren't born into wealth. It was their faith and obedience that made the difference, keeping their hearts soft and their minds firm. Faith and obedience are things we can all build and develop.

After the second miraculous battle, my stripling warriors and the rest of the Nephite armies kept at it, doing our best to expel the Lamanites from the western part of the nation. The strongest Lamanite outpost was the city of Manti, a Nephite city that had been taken by the Lamanites and made their headquarters on the western front. Digging the Lamanites out would be no small task.

The task was made more difficult by the lack of provisions.

Notwithstanding our great success and the miraculous preservation of the stripling warriors, all the Nephite armies in our area received very little support from Zarahemla. We were about to perish for the want of food. We finally received a small convoy with a few more men and some provisions, but that was all.

My men and I began to fear that Zarahemla was mired in intrigue and dissent. I knew discord would bring the judgments of God against us. "Therefore we did pour out our souls in prayer to God, that He would strengthen us and deliver us out of the hands of our enemies, yea, and also give us strength that we might retain our cities, and our lands, and our possessions, for the support of our people. Yea, and it came to pass that the Lord their God did visit us with assurances that he would deliver us; yea, insomuch that he did speak peace to our souls, and did grant unto us great faith, and did cause us that we should hope for our deliverance in him."[57]

What do you think it means to be "visited with assurances"? For us it didn't mean God told us exactly what to do or how we were going to survive. Instead, He comforted us and He visited us with assurances that somehow, someway, we would be delivered. He filled us with faith and with the Spirit.

You can have these same assurances if you pray. Earlier I told you that the only thing special about the stripling warriors was their faith, and that faith like theirs can be developed. Now you know that prayer is the key to developing faith. When we pour out our souls in prayer to God, it unlocks the blessings He already has waiting for us. God knows what we want, but more importantly, He knows what we need. We just have to

57. Alma 58:10–11.

ask. He can give us the "go and do" attitude, and He can assure us that everything will work out, even when the odds are stacked against us.

So we were encouraged, though there was no earthly reason to be so. Thus encouraged, we worked on a plan, a variation of what had worked before. This time, we hid a small number of men in the forest around the city of Manti while the rest camped out near the city gates. The guards of the Lamanites surveyed the ragtag army at their doors, and our sad and sorry state led their captains to decide to mount a quick and decisive offensive.

The Lamanite army emerged *en masse*, hoping to overwhelm the much weaker Nephite army with sheer speed. According to plan, the Nephite army took off into the woods, leading the Lamanite army after them. The Nephite army had to stay close, or they knew the Lamanites wouldn't take the bait. In the meantime, the small group of soldiers we left behind came out of hiding and quickly defeated the few Lamanite guards left behind. The first stage of the plan was a success.

The second stage called for the pursued army to change their course. In a body, they began to move as quickly as possible toward the land of Zarahemla. Because many of the members of the Lamanite army were also Nephite dissenters, they quickly realized the change in direction meant they were now heading directly toward Zarahemla. The Lamanites began to fear they were being led into a trap. *Surely there is a larger Nephite army heading our way from Zarahemla!* they thought.

As evening fell, the Lamanites halted their march and set up camp. They decided to abandon their pursuit and return to the city of Manti first thing in the morning. This decision perfectly set up the third stage of the plan. Unfortunately, we knew all too well there was no help waiting for us on the road to Zarahemla, but the

Lamanites didn't. Since there was no reason for us to continue in that direction, we circled widely around the Lamanite camp and continued our march through the night, arriving back at the city of Manti early in the morning. When the Lamanite army returned later that day, they found the city of Manti filled with our army. The Lamanites were "exceedingly astonished and struck with great fear, insomuch that they did flee into the wilderness . . . and out of this quarter of the land entirely."[58]

It was nice that the Lamanites left, but the collateral damage was heavy: they carried off with them many Nephite women and children. Losing these good, faithful women and children was very difficult for their families. Sadly, that loss is symbolic of the suffering caused by giving in to temptation and serious sin. The damage done to our families can be significant. For example, when people on paper or screens become objects to be used, it is only a matter of time before real people become mere objects as well.

In addition, people who engage in serious sin without seeking to repent will, over time, seek more and more dangerous and risky behavior. This leads to more selfish behavior and more violent behavior. At first the damage is limited just to you, but soon it extends to your family.

The war was full of highs and lows. It's hard to explain the conflict of emotions caused by seeing the miracles of my stripling warriors, contrasted with the neglect of our government. It was painful. That is why I wrote all this down and sent it to Moroni. I needed his help. I needed someone else to rejoice in the good things that had happened, and also to know about the hard things as well. Hopefully, the stripling warriors' story will be a blessing to you.

Here comes Moroni—and look, his man bun is back!

58. Alma 58:29–30.

CAPTAIN'S LOG
• The Spirit will visit us with assurances
• We can use strategy to defeat temptation
• Mothers are awesome! Obey them!

CHAPTER 14

MORONI AND HIS MAN BUN

MORONI: Hopefully you found Helaman's words inspiring. I sure did. Look at my man bun! Helaman reminded me that I may have been too harsh on our man-bun-wearing friends, especially since I was the first one to make it look good. So I'm bringing the man bun back!

HELAMAN: Moroni, the man bun is already back. Lots of guys have been wearing man buns lately. Ask your readers.

MORONI: Thank you, Helaman, for that very rousing story! Time to go. Shoo! Shoo! Off you go!

Okay, where were we?! Right, the stripling warriors! When I finished reading Helaman's letter, I rejoiced because of his welfare and success, and that of his stripling warriors. I made their stories known unto all the people in the land round about me, that they might rejoice also. I also immediately sent a letter to our chief judge, Pahoran, asking him to send men and provisions to Helaman right away. Instead of receiving a response from Pahoran, I received word that a large city we had recently retaken, Nephihah, had just been destroyed by the Lamanites. Weeks earlier, I asked Pahoran to send reinforcements to that city. I discovered none were sent. As a result, most of those left to maintain the city lost their lives in the Lamanite offensive.

I began to believe that my letter to Pahoran regarding Helaman's needs would be similarly ignored. I became exceedingly sorrowful, and I confess that for the first time, I began to doubt, because of the wickedness of the people, whether we would fall to the Lamanites. In fact, all my captains began to doubt and marvel because of the wickedness of our people, due to the success of the Lamanites over us.[59] And I began to think Pahoran was responsible. He asked if he could come tell his version of the events, so here he is.

59. Alma 59:12.

CHAPTER 15

PAHORAN'S SIDE OF THE STORY

PAHORAN: Hey, guys, Pahoran here! Captain Moroni brought me along to tell my side of the story. He still feels bad for being a little harsh with me, and he thought this might help make up for it. He was wrong.

Just kidding! I have never been mad at Moroni. I *completely* understand why he threatened to kill me!

So, one morning I was awakened very early by a messenger who brought me a letter from Moroni. I quickly opened it and read that the armies of Moroni and Helaman were both suffering from hunger, thirst, fatigue, and all manner of afflictions of every kind. What was worse, a great many soldiers and civilians had perished by the sword of the Lamanites.

Moroni wanted to know why no additional men and provisions had been provided. Wow, if he only knew! If he only knew that I was reading his letter in exile, in the land of Gideon, far from Zarahemla. If he only knew how happy I had been just a few weeks earlier, when I'd heard that Nephihah had been retaken by Nephite armies! Moroni had written to

me then, asking for men and provisions to be sent to Nephihah so that it might be preserved.

Both Moroni and I knew that cities were much easier to maintain than to retake, so Nephihah must be fortified! I quickly convened the council of lower judges and explained the situation. When I informed them that Nephihah had been retaken, the lower judges were genuinely surprised, but it was an odd kind of surprised—more like a disappointed surprised than a happy surprised. I thought this was curious, but I pressed forward, discussing the need for additional troops and supplies. When I finished, there was a long silence. Finally, one of the other judges cleared his throat and said, "We're not sending more."

"Excuse me?" I replied, beginning to be astonished. The man's name was Pachus, and I looked at him in bewilderment.

Pachus continued, his voice rising menacingly, "I said, we're not sending more. No more men, no more supplies, no more nothing." Simultaneously, several armed men rushed into the room from the front, and my guards grabbed me and pulled me out through the back. We barely made it out with our lives, and the only reason we did was that the streets were crowded with the bustle of the afternoon market. We were able to get lost in the masses.

For the next few days, my life was in constant danger. I didn't know whom I could trust. It was so difficult just staying alive that it was nearly impossible to organize the freemen. You see, the king-men had risen again!

When I read Moroni's account of the sufferings of the Nephite army, it gnawed at my soul. But there were many who rejoiced in Moroni's afflictions. In fact, the sufferings and setbacks of the Nephite armies encouraged the king-men and helped them to use great flattery to lead away the hearts of many people.[60]

I sent word several times to Moroni, but I knew the Lamanite army was aware of Moroni's whereabouts and was intercepting every message they could. So I wrote a proclamation and sent it out

60. See Alma 61:4.

to every Nephite city possible, and then I prayed that my letters would arrive. Then, I prayed that my prayer would work! I knew prayer was our only hope.

When I was a boy, I often heard my father and other church leaders say that we should pray always. I admit that this didn't make a lot of sense to me as a kid. Was I supposed to walk around with my head bowed all the time, running into things? Should I pray about whether to drink chocolate milk or regular milk? (The answer is always chocolate, by the way.)

When I was an older teenager, I was reading the words of Nephi one day and it all made sense. In 2 Nephi 32:9 it reads, "But behold, I say unto you that ye must pray always, and not faint; that ye must not perform any thing unto the Lord save in the first place ye shall pray unto the Father in the name of Christ, that he will consecrate thy performance unto thee, that thy performance may be for the welfare of thy soul." Once again, the beginning of that verse says that we should pray always. I still remember sighing in frustration when I saw that. But then it says we "must not perform anything unto the Lord save in the first place ye shall pray." I realized that I'm not performing the choice between chocolate milk and regular milk unto the Lord. He doesn't care which flavor I choose. There are a lot of things we do every day that aren't performed unto the Lord. I still remember the relief I felt that the Lord didn't expect me to pray over every little thing!

The next part of the verse, however, is even more important. It says that we should pray that the Lord "will consecrate thy performance unto thee, that thy performance may be for the welfare of thy soul." I began to think about all the things I do that I would like consecrated for the welfare of my soul. To "consecrate" means to bless or make sacred. What things do you do or "perform" that you would like blessed or made sacred? Your schoolwork? Your scripture study? Your journal writing? Your athletic events? Your interaction with your family and friends? I realized that day, reading that scripture, that I performed a lot of things unto the Lord that I wasn't praying about. So I began to pray! Not every waking moment, but a lot more frequently!

Even as an adult, after a long day of chief judge-ing, I would often stand on my doorstep and pause for a moment before opening the door to my home. Standing there for a moment with my head bowed, I would silently offer a prayer asking God to consecrate my performance as a husband and a father for the welfare of my family. That prayer would often help me make the sometimes difficult transition from work life to home life. I'm sure it will do the same for you if you remember to say a silent prayer on your way home from school.

So, as I was saying earlier, after I sent out that proclamation, I prayed, and it worked! Freemen began flocking to us daily, bringing their weapons in defense of their country and their freedom. So many came that the king-men feared to come against us. But I was conflicted. The king-men were Nephites. I did not want to go to battle against Nephites if I could avoid it. I knew that many of them were confused, that they were seduced by the flattery of Ammoron and his traitors in the Nephite government. I even learned Pachus had been corresponding with Ammoron, and Amalickiah before him, for several years! Pachus had been promised that if he would turn over Zarahemla to the Lamanites, he would be made the ruler over Zarahemla by Ammoron himself!

I knew that Ammoron and the king-men had corrupted, flattered, and threatened many into submission. I did not want to destroy life wantonly. I had not given up hope for a peaceful resolution, and I was praying for guidance. Then I received Moroni's letter. After telling me what I already knew, that many in the Nephite government only cared for power and wealth, Moroni then said, "Behold, the Lord saith unto me: If those whom ye have appointed your governors do not repent of their sins and iniquities, ye shall go up to battle against them."[61] When I read that, the Spirit testified to me that this was how bad things were. There was no way to engage the democratic process when I had been run out of town and the king-men were in an alliance with the Lamanites. We had to fight.

I quickly wrote a response to Moroni and sent it off, fervently praying it would make it through to him. I told him that I did not find joy in his great afflictions, but that they grieved my soul. I said, "In your epistle you have censured me, but it mattereth not; I am not angry, but do rejoice in the greatness of your heart. I, Pahoran, do not seek for power, save only to retain my judgment seat that I may preserve the rights and the liberty of my people. My soul standeth fast in that liberty in the which God hath made us free."[62]

61. Alma 60:33.
62. Alma 61:9.

I told Moroni to leave part of his army in the charge of Lehi and Teancum and to take the rest and come to me and my growing army. I told him to gather together whatsoever force he could upon his march so that we might go speedily against the dissenters. And Moroni received the message! My prayer was answered. Moroni took a small number of men and began his march toward the land of Gideon. Everywhere he went, he raised the title of liberty, inviting all who would defend freedom to join his throng, "and it came to pass that thousands did flock unto his standard."[63]

Moroni arrived at the land of Gideon and did unite his forces with my own, making us exceedingly strong. We wasted no time marching down to Zarahemla to give the men of Pachus battle. It was a short affair with very little loss of life. Pachus was slain and the rest of his men taken prisoners. Those who would not stand for freedom from the Lamanites were put to death. Once again, the king-men had been defeated![64]

The first thing Moroni and I did was send an army of six thousand men with supplies to Helaman. Then we sent as many men and supplies to Lehi and Teancum. Finally, Moroni and I set off with a large army to Nephihah. It was time to set things right. I had no idea how "right" things were about to be.

Moroni and I were determined to overthrow the Lamanites in Nephihah. On our way, we ran into an envoy of Lamanites carrying weapons and food. We hit them so hard and fast that four thousand of them surrendered and pleaded with us to let them go live

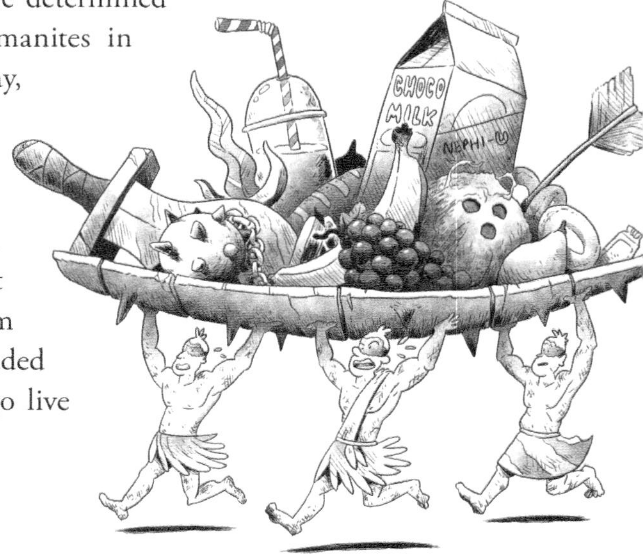

63. Alma 62:3–5.
64. Alma 62:7–9.

with the people of Ammon. What?! This was a complete surprise to me, but Moroni wasn't surprised at all. You see, after he received Helaman's letter, he published the news of the stripling warriors' success far and wide. Everyone in his camp thought his goal was to inspire the Nephites in that quarter of the land. Nope. Moroni wanted the Lamanite armies to hear about their brethren. The people of Ammon were famous among the Lamanites. They were famous for their conversion and for their unwillingness to fight. They were famous for joining the Nephites. And now they were famous for their sons' preservation in war. The Lamanite armies hadn't heard about the stripling warriors only from Moroni's news reports, but also from Lamanite soldiers who had run for their lives from the fierceness of the stripling warriors!

When these four thousand Lamanite prisoners realized they had been captured by Captain Moroni, they remembered what he had done at the battle with Zerahemnah, they remembered what the stripling warriors had been doing on the western front, and they began begging for mercy. They didn't just beg for mercy—they begged for citizenship! They wanted whatever the people of Ammon had. So Moroni gave it to them. He trusted those Lamanites implicitly. He didn't send them to the land of Jershon with armed guards; he sent them with helpful guides.

Do you realize what a miracle this was? These were real people and real events. These Lamanites surrendered and then begged and pleaded to join the families of the stripling warriors. Many of them had seen those warriors fight, seen their obedience and their goodness. Those Lamanites wanted what the stripling warriors had. This can happen to you too! As you live obediently and keep yourself clean, others around you—even those who seem drenched in sin—will want what you have. They will want it so badly that they will be willing to give away all their sins to have it. Never underestimate the power of a righteous example—the power of *your* righteous example.

You know, Moroni once confided in me the source of his inspiration to offer the Lamanites mercy. He reminded me of the story of the prophet Elisha in the Old Testament, and how the Syrian army surrounded Elisha so they could kill him. Elisha's servant was afraid, but Elisha said, "Fear not: for they that be with us are more than they that be with them."[65] Elisha then prayed that the Lord would open the eyes of the young man, "and he saw: and, behold, the mountain was full of horses and chariots of fire round about Elisha."[66] Now, you have likely heard that part of the story before, but do you remember the rest? Elisha then prayed that the Syrian army would be struck with blindness, which they were, and then he led them to the king of Israel. The king of Israel asked Elisha if he should smite the Syrians, but instead Elisha told the king to "set bread and water before them, that they may eat and drink, and go to their master."[67] So the king listened to Elisha and "prepared great provision for them: and when they had eaten and drunk, he sent them away, and they went to their master. So the bands of Syria came no more into the land of Israel."[68] Instead of destroying the Syrian army when they had them captive, the Israelites fed them, and the Syrians did not return to fight. Captain Moroni told me that this story really impacted him. If mercy could work for the Israelites, why couldn't it work for the Nephites?

Of course, now we know that mercy *did* work. Thousands of Lamanites joined the people of Ammon in Jershon, and we continued our march to Nephihah. In Nephihah, Moroni had the idea to

65. 2 Kings 6:16.
66. 2 Kings 6:17.
67. 2 Kings 6:22.
68. 2 Kings 6:23.

climb the walls in the middle of the night and let our entire army down into the city while the Lamanites slept. When the Lamanites awoke in the morning to find us waiting for them inside the city, many fled. Some were killed, some escaped, but most were surrounded. Once again, Moroni began to talk to the prisoners. He didn't talk to them like they were war criminals, he didn't talk to them like they were murderers, and he didn't even talk to them like they were Lamanites. He spoke to them like brothers. He explained that four thousand of their brethren had just left for the land of Jershon, and he asked if they were interested in joining them.[69]

"Therefore, all the prisoners of the Lamanites did join the people of Ammon, and did begin to labor exceedingly—tilling the ground, raising all manner of grain, and flocks and herds of every kind; and thus were the Nephites relieved from a great burden; yea, insomuch that they were relieved from all the prisoners of the Lamanites."[70]

In retaking Nephihah, our armies were greatly strengthened by the many Nephite prisoners the Lamanites had been holding

69. Alma 62:28.
70. Alma 62:29.

there. Moreover, the Lamanite army was suddenly reduced by thousands—not because they had been killed, but because they had been converted.

The addition to our armies, combined with the drastic reduction in the Lamanite armies, created a new balance of power. We began chasing the Lamanites from city to city, further and further from our capital and closer and closer to their own lands. During that chase, we met up with the armies of Lehi and Teancum, joining them with our own. Finally, the entire Lamanite army was gathered together in one body in one city. Ironically, it was the city of Moroni, named for our captain.

We were so weary from the speediness of our march that we did not hold a war council that night after making camp. Strategy would have to wait until morning. Or so we thought . . .

CHAPTER 16

TEANCUM IN HIS OWN WORDS

TEANCUM: Have a seat, Pahoran. My turn.

Finally, I get to tell my story! Moroni always says he tells my story better than I do, but he already told about how I broke Zerahemnah's sword *and* about how I killed Amalickiah. I would like to tell the final chapter of my story. It's the final chapter, you see, because it's where I sneak into the Lamanite camp, kill Ammoron, and lose my life in the process. And yes, I am wearing something of a ninja-style tracksuit. Moroni said I look kind of silly, but I like to be comfortable. He should just be glad I'm not wearing velour. Man, I love velour.

Moroni makes a big deal about how I took someone with me when I killed Amalickiah. You may be wondering why I chose to go it alone the night I killed Ammoron. I would like to explain myself.

In the beginning of this book, when you first met Moroni, he said he believed there were a lot of reasons Mormon included so much of this war in the gold plates. Amalickiah is a great analogy for temptation and sin, but the analogy is not 100 percent perfect. Every time you read through the Book of Mormon, you don't have to read the story of Captain Moroni and Amalickiah only through the lens of temptation; in fact, we all hope you don't. Overcoming sin is important, but there are many more layers and lessons in any scripture story than just one.

My story is a good example of these different layers. Applying the lens of temptation, there is a very easy lesson to learn from my story: Don't try to overcome it alone! When I attacked Amalickiah at night, I wasn't alone. Not only were we successful in our mission, but we returned safely back to camp. However, when I attacked Ammoron, I went alone. Even though I was able to kill Ammoron, I didn't make it back alive. While it is true that no one can or should try to overcome serious sin like substance abuse or pornography alone, my own story is more complicated. It isn't accurate to say I was some lone wolf who went rogue when I went after Ammoron.

You see, no one knew better than I how risky my attack against Ammoron would be. My stealth attack against Amalickiah was famous among the Lamanites and the Nephites. In the intervening years, many captured Lamanites talked openly about the impact of Amalickiah's killing and about how much more careful Ammoron was as a result.

Ammoron changed tents almost every night and severely punished any guards he caught asleep at their posts. In fact, Ammoron's nighttime paranoia became legendary among the Lamanites, so much so that it was well known even among the civilian Nephite population. The result was that for a long time I never seriously considered attempting a stealth attack against Ammoron.

Until that fateful night at the city of Moroni.

That night, I suspected Ammoron's army was in greater disarray than ever before. They had been retreating steadily day after day and suffering significant losses from both casualties and deserters. On that particular evening, there was an obvious and dramatic decrease in organization and morale among the Lamanites. It dawned on me that there may be a small window of opportunity here, one that I might be able to exploit. I seriously considered bringing someone with me, but knowing how paranoid Ammoron was, I couldn't bear the thought of asking any of my friends and brothers to take the risk. I had seen too much death already. I just couldn't do it. So I went alone.

It was the dead of night when I silently approached the city walls that protected Ammoron and his army. I found a section of the wall that was shielded by foliage and far from the guard towers. I climbed the wall with the help of a rope I had brought. Once I reached the top, right away I could tell that my suspicions were accurate. There were fewer guard fires than normal, and the camp was a mess. I began to circle the wall slowly, taking special care to stay out of sight. I was looking for anything out of the ordinary—one tent with extra security, for example. Perhaps Ammoron had been careless just this once.

I had my javelin with me, and I was a pretty good aim. I just needed to get close. As I moved around the wall, there were different sections of the city. I had to let myself down to get a closer look and then climb back up to get to a different section. I noticed a greater concentration of tents in the area furthest from the city gate. Then I saw a guard fire set right in front

of a tent—a tent that had obviously seen a lot of wear but that was still noticeably larger and of higher quality than the others. I didn't think much of it at first—Ammoron was known to set up decoy tents. Then I looked closer at the fire. There were three men sitting at the fire, not speaking a word. I could hardly believe my eyes—one of them was Ammoron! It was the middle of the night; I never imagined he would still be awake. He was just sitting there with his guards, staring blankly into the flames.

So I sat, too. I knew Ammoron would eventually get up and go into one of the tents. Finally, half an hour later, he stood up and wordlessly walked to a different tent, not the nicer one I had noticed earlier. The stories we'd heard about his paranoia were obviously true. The tent he got into was small, and from the nearby firelight, I was able to see from his shadow approximately where he lay down inside. Now I just needed to wait a bit longer, hope Ammoron fell asleep, and come up with a plan.

After another half hour of sitting in the shadows, I decided it was time to act. The Lamanite guards had their backs to the rear wall and would anticipate that any disturbances would come from in front of them, where passageways led to other areas of the city. As luck would have it, there were no guards on the back wall, so I could let myself down right behind the guards. Yes, you heard me right: I was moving in closer to them.

I found a large rock on the narrow stretch on top of the wall and tucked it away. Then I let down my rope and began to slowly descend right behind the guards. When I was still above them in the air, a few feet up and a few feet behind, I took my rock and threw it across the courtyard

toward the other entrance. The rock clattered to the ground and the guards looked up with a start.

The two guards by the fire immediately stood up to investigate, walking quickly away from me. I didn't waste any time. Now that their backs were turned to me and they were moving away, I dropped quietly to the ground and headed toward my quarry. In no time, I was among the tents, walking around them and in between them. I knew I didn't have much more time, especially if I wanted to get away. I was about ten yards from Ammoron's tent, on the side where I knew he was lying down. I raised my javelin and threw it with all my strength.

The javelin ripped through the tent, and almost immediately there was a piercing scream. I hit Ammoron! I didn't know where I had hit him, and I didn't have time to check. Without even turning to look at the guards, I took off through the tents back toward my cord, which was still hanging from the wall. If I could just get to the top, I might have a chance to escape.

I didn't make it to the top.

I got close, but an arrow hit my back. Thankfully, it was a quick end. I died not knowing whether I had been successful in ending Ammoron's life. I died not knowing if my effort had made any difference at all. It reminds me a little bit of another Book of Mormon prophet you may have heard of, whose name was Abinadi.

During my days on earth, I spent a lot of time thinking about Abinadi.

Abinadi stood up to wicked King Noah and his high priests. And while it must have meant a lot to Abinadi to see Alma the Elder try to defend him, as far as Abinadi knew, Alma was the only one who did. The last Abinadi ever saw of Alma was his back as Alma fled, the king's guards in close pursuit. Abinadi died not knowing if Alma had even survived that chase.

But Alma did survive, hiding himself from the king's searches and teaching whoever would listen at the Waters of Mormon. The prophet Mormon was named after the Waters of Mormon, and the Waters of Mormon were always considered a sacred place of restoration by the Nephites. The Nephites taught that the Waters of Mormon is where the Church was restored among Alma's people.[71]

Through Joseph Smith, the Lord restored the gospel once again in your day. Over the years, many people have persecuted the Church, and early persecutors called it the "Mormon Church" like it was an insult. But the joke is on them, because the name "Mormon" doesn't just celebrate the work Mormon did to bring you the record of the Nephites, but that name also celebrates the restoration that Alma helped bring to pass at the Waters of Mormon. By calling us the "Mormon Church," our detractors only highlight that we are the restored Church of Jesus Christ, just as in Alma's day. But, of course, *we* know better. We know the Savior himself taught that this is His Church, and it bears His name.[72] We didn't call it "Alma's Church" during Alma's

71. 3 Nephi 5:12.
72. 3 Nephi 27:8.

day, and we don't call it the "Mormon Church" today. This is The Church of Jesus Christ of Latter-day Saints.

The restoration at the Waters of Mormon would never have happened without Abinadi. Alma was Abinadi's only convert, and when Alma arrived in Zarahemla, it was he who King Mosiah put in charge of establishing the Church of Christ among the Nephites. It was Alma who convinced King Mosiah to change the government from a monarchy to elected judges. Then Alma's own son, Alma the Younger, became the first chief judge. You have already met the prophet Helaman; he is the grandson of Alma the Elder.

Abinadi's death led to so much good, but he never knew it in life. Remember this when you serve a mission or do any missionary work. Abinadi, perhaps one of the greatest missionaries in the Book of Mormon, died having led only one person to conversion. And he may not even have known it. Many have served honorably with little to no outward success when they complete their mission. But the number of baptisms speaks nothing of the seeds they planted when they served. In so many cases, some seeds take root later on. You never know—maybe *your* efforts will lead to an "Alma the Elder" who ignites the conversion of thousands.

Abinadi's testimony and death were not in vain. I was inspired by Abinadi's example, and I always tried to be the best soldier I could so that if ever I died in battle, my death would not be in vain. And it wasn't. I know now that the wound I gave Ammoron was fatal. That next morning, Moroni felt the best way to honor my death was to take advantage of the chaos my efforts caused among the Lamanites. Moroni marched in with his armies at dawn and defeated the Lamanites. Many were killed, and the rest fled out of the land and back to the Lamanite cities. The war was over.

Moroni still gives me a hard time. He says I should have waited until morning and we would have destroyed the Lamanites anyway. Perhaps, but perhaps not. What I am sure of is that Ammoron would not have stopped until Moroni was dead, and even if the Nephite army won the next day's battle, there was no guarantee Ammoron wouldn't have escaped. Whenever I point that out to Moroni, he awkwardly changes the subject.

So you see, while it is completely true that you should seek help to defeat serious temptation, like I did when I killed Amalickiah, the analogy doesn't completely capture my experience with Ammoron. Your bishop is not going to be put in danger if you ask for help: it's a different situation. If there is anything you take away from my story, it should be that we can't always see the good that our righteous choices lead to. I couldn't, and Abinadi couldn't. If you wait until you know the results before acting, you'll never act, and you'll never produce righteous results.

If you need help overcoming temptation, ask for help today. Nothing makes Satan madder than quick, decisive, righteous action. And I love ticking Satan off!

CHAPTER 17

MORONI'S BEST FRIEND

MORONI: Thank you, Teancum. For everything.

We were all very sad to lose Teancum but very thankful the war was over. Can you believe the evil efforts of Amalickiah, Ammoron, and the king-men? These were all Nephites—Nephites seeking after power and riches instead of righteousness.

Mormon said it best when he wrote the following about Amalickiah: "Yea, and we also see the great wickedness one very wicked man can cause to take place among the children of men. Yea, we see that Amalickiah, because he was a man of cunning device and a man of many flattering words, that he led away the hearts of many people to do wickedly; yea, and to seek to destroy the church of God, and to destroy the foundation of liberty which God had granted unto them, or which blessing God had sent upon the face of the land for the righteous' sake."[73]

In the midst of the war, all the dissension, and the never-ending betrayals and intrigues, I ran into Lehi one day. Lehi had been with me in the more part of my battles, but at that particular time, we were in separate areas

73. Alma 46:9–10.

fighting separate contingents of the Lamanite army. We hadn't seen each other in a while, and I confess that when we hugged, I almost began to cry. Mormon recorded the following about Lehi and me: "Now behold, this Lehi was a man who had been with Moroni in the more part of all his battles; and he was a man like unto Moroni, and they rejoiced in each other's safety; yea, they were beloved by each other, and also beloved by all the people of Nephi."[74] I knew I didn't have to worry about Lehi or his faith; he never left you to imagine or guess whose side he was on. Lehi did not seek for power and wealth. He was quick to testify and quicker to serve.

Because of Lehi's faith and goodness, I felt safe with him. There were so many others during this difficult time period with whom I did not feel safe. Do you have friends like Lehi? Friends who are not afraid to show their faith, not afraid to stand up for what is right? Are you a friend *like* Lehi? Do you support others in their righteousness? Do you stand up for goodness and purity? There is nothing like having friends like this.

I saved Lehi for last. He was my closest friend and confidant, and I know he has great things to share with you. Lehi, the floor is yours . . .

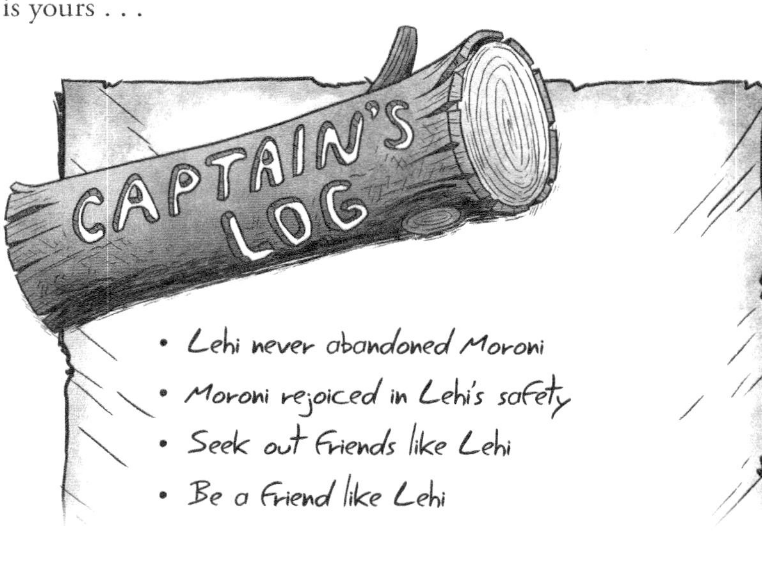

74. Alma 53:2.

CHAPTER 18

LEHI'S CHOICE

LEHI: Er, wow, thank you, Moroni. I've always really liked this, um, *particular* floor. It's, ah, so nice of you to *give* it to me!

MORONI: Don't mention it. And don't forget to mop it up when you're finished, wise guy.

LEHI: Like Moroni said, he and I are best friends. But it could have gone a different way. When my father retired as chief captain of the Nephite armies, most people thought I would replace him. I admit I thought so as well. When Moroni was called instead, I didn't quite know how to react. It hurt my pride. So I went to my knees and talked it over with my Father in Heaven. I was honest about my pride, and I prayed for help to support God's will. After much prayer and fasting, I soon found myself in a leadership meeting in which Captain Moroni was outlining his plans. I'll never forget it: I felt the Spirit so strongly! It wasn't that I was impressed with his ideas. It was more than that.

The Spirit witnessed to me that Moroni had been chosen and prepared, and I felt the love the Lord had for him. There was no looking back.

Not long after, Amalickiah approached me in secret. He hadn't come out in open rebellion yet, but I know now he was already grooming his supporters. He knew I had been passed over, and he tried to subtly drive a wedge between Moroni and me. He thought I would be bitter, that I would have hard feelings against Moroni. He was wrong.

I had learned from Laman and Lemuel's bad example. You see, Nephi was their *younger* brother, and that really bothered Laman and Lemuel. They couldn't handle Nephi's goodness and righteousness. Laman thought that since he was the oldest, he should be in charge. But Laman wasn't willing to pay the price to earn the position. Laman did not listen to his parents, he did not spend time in the scriptures, and he did not pray. As a result, Laman did not

come to know God or His plan for him.

I've always believed that if Laman had made different choices and embraced Nephi's goodness, things would have turned out very differently for him. With better teaching from their parents, Laman's children may have made different choices, and perhaps some of them would have become great spiritual leaders. You can actually see this happen in Joseph Smith's family. Joseph's older brother, Hyrum, humbled himself and accepted Joseph's position with God. Hyrum was never a prophet, but he always supported his brother. This unquestioned faith and loyalty was clear to Hyrum's children. Not surprisingly, Hyrum's son, Joseph F. Smith, later became a prophet. Hyrum's grandson, Joseph Fielding Smith, became a prophet as well. I suspect something similar may have happened in the lives of Laman and Lemuel, had they lived as Hyrum lived.

In any event, I decided very soon after Moroni's appointment that I was not going to be a Laman. Because of that decision, I saved my soul, made the best friend of my life, and participated in one of the greatest periods of Nephite history. Yeah, I'd say I made the right choice! By the way, I think I should tell you that Captain Moroni is actually allowed to call anyone "Buttercup." It's in his contract from when he was made Captain of the Nephite armies . . . chapter 4, article 7: "Captain Moroni may call anyone Buttercup as he sees fit." He tried calling me Buttercup once. Without getting into too many details, I'll just say it only happened once. **wink**

Remember when Moroni talked about the people of Limhi earlier? About how he got the idea for armor from the Jaredite relics Limhi brought back? There's another part of Limhi's story that I want to talk about. You see, Limhi and his people probably never should have lived among the Lamanites in the first place. Do you remember why the Nephites first came to Zarahemla? The Nephites used to live in the land of Nephi, but the Lamanites there were getting too numerous and the battles too frequent. The king of the Nephites was named King Mosiah I. He was the father of King Benjamin and the grandfather of King Mosiah II. King Mosiah I was prompted by the Spirit to leave the land of Nephi and to take all those who were faithful to Christ with him. So they left, and after many days, they found the land of Zarahemla.[75]

After a few years in Zarahemla, a group of men was sent back to the land of Nephi to scout out the Lamanites and see what they were doing. Part of that group wanted to do a surprise attack on the Lamanites to keep them from ever coming to war against the Nephites again. Another part thought that was the wrong idea.

There was a battle, and many Nephites perished. The rest returned home to tell that tale to the families of the dead men.[76]

Zeniff was the leader of the men who did not want to destroy the Lamanites. Perhaps he missed the land where he had grown up, or perhaps he felt guilty over the battle in the wilderness. Whatever the reason, Zeniff decided to go back and resettle the land of Nephi with as many people as wanted go with him. And many people wanted to. Zarahemla was new to the Nephites, and so were its people. There was a language barrier, and the surroundings were unfamiliar. While it is understandable that people would want to go back, it is also pretty clear that they should have followed their leader, King Mosiah, and his prompting to stay in Zarahemla.[77]

75. Omni 1:12–13.
76. Mosiah 9:2.
77. 3 Nephi 5:12.

Surprisingly, Zeniff and his people were accepted by the Lamanites and allowed to dwell in the land Shiloh. To his great credit, Zeniff soon redoubled his efforts to follow the Lord and keep His commandments, and his people did the same. As a result, they were forgiven and experienced many years of peace among the Lamanites. They even successfully rebuffed the attacks of the Lamanites through the strength of the Lord.

Unfortunately, Zeniff chose his son Noah to replace him as king upon his death. Noah was nothing like his father, and under Noah's rule the people quickly embraced wickedness. Noah cast off the righteous priests of his father, including Abinadi, and named new, wicked priests, including Alma the Elder. As a result of the wickedness of the people, the disobedience of Zeniff to the revelations of King Mosiah came back to haunt them. Not only did they no longer receive the protection of the Lord, but they now found themselves surrounded by Lamanites and all alone. Teancum has already talked to you about Abinadi, so I don't need to go into that part of the story, but after Alma the Elder left with the believers and wicked King Noah was killed, Limhi was left in charge of those who remained. Limhi was one of King Noah's sons, but he was not like his father. Limhi knew concerning his father's sins, and he did not want to repeat them.[78]

Limhi's people continued to live among the Lamanites, but basically as their slaves. They were required to pay a large tax to the Lamanites or be killed. This felt very unfair to Limhi's people, and on three separate occasions they tried to free themselves from their Lamanite bondage. Each time, they suffered huge losses. Finally, they were forced to humble themselves to the dust and accept their situation. It was also during this time that the wicked priests of King Noah (except for Alma the Elder), who were hiding in the wilderness, stole the daughters of the Lamanites and caused additional destruction among the people of Limhi.

78. Mosiah 19:17.

Eventually, Ammon showed up with a crew from Zarahemla. This wasn't the Ammon who later converted many Lamanites, but a man by the same name who was a native of Zarahemla and who knew his way around the country.

You may recall how the people of Limhi freed themselves, by getting the Lamanite guards drunk and then escaping out through the back way of the city. The record states, "And now it came to pass when the Lamanites had found that the people of Limhi had departed out of the land by night, that they sent an army into the wilderness to pursue them; and after they had pursued them two days, they could no longer follow their tracks; therefore they were lost in the wilderness."[79]

I want you to remember how the Lamanites could no longer follow the people of Limhi's tracks. We'll talk about that more later. In the meantime, the Lamanite army that was lost chasing the people of Limhi soon became even more lost. During their wanderings, they first found the wicked priests of King Noah as well as the Lamanite daughters whom they had carried off. Next, they found Alma the Elder and his people living peacefully in the land of Helam.

Remember, many years had passed since Alma the Elder had repented of his sins and begun teaching the word of the Lord. Then, all of a sudden, the Lamanite army was upon them, together with Amulon and the other wicked priests of King Noah. Amulon and his cohort didn't know Alma as a man of God; they knew him as a wicked priest. Amulon and his buddies had never repented and did not give Alma any credit for doing so.

Somehow, Amulon obtained favor in the sight of the Lamanite leader and was made ruler over Alma and the land of Helam. Amulon did not like Alma and his people, and he began to exercise unrighteous dominion over them. Imagine how painful this must have been for Alma the Elder, to have his past sinful life suddenly brought back before him. He had been keeping the commandments

---

79. Mosiah 22:15–16.

for years, but Amulon threw his past right back into his face and despised him for trying to be better.

Think of how disheartening it must have felt for Alma to have to interact with Amulon, who knew of his sins and would not accept his repentance or see him in a new way. Imagine Alma's emotions when he found out that the reason the Lamanites had found him was because the people of Limhi had escaped. Alma and his people had repented years before the people of Limhi, but the people of Limhi were liberated first. Do you think Alma's faith in God was tested? He and his people repented long before the people of Limhi, but now the people of Limhi were safe and free, and he was not. In fact, Alma found himself in bondage in part *because* of the people of Limhi. Remember, the Lamanite army became lost chasing the escaping people of Limhi and then happened upon Alma and his people.

One of your modern-day Apostles, a great man named Elder Neil A. Maxwell, said that "irony is the hard crust on the bread of adversity."[80] Alma was eating that bread. In fact, the opening scripture Elder Maxwell uses for his talk is taken directly from Alma's story with Amulon: "Nevertheless the Lord seeth fit to chasten his people; yea, he trieth their patience and their faith."[81] Even though Alma and his people repented long before the people of Limhi, Limhi's people were now free, and Alma was under Amulon's thumb. As Amulon began to treat Alma and his people more and more violently, the people began to pray more and more mightily. Finally, Amulon commanded that anyone

80. "Irony: The Crust on the Bread of Adversity," *Ensign*, May 1989.
81. Mosiah 23:21.

praying out loud would be put to death. So the people began to pour out their minds and their hearts to God silently. And God did visit them in their afflictions and did make their burdens light. In fact, so light were the burdens made that the people began to *submit cheerfully* and with all patience to their burdens.[82]

Finally, the Lord visited Alma and told him to prepare his people for escape. Alma and his people spent all night gathering their flocks and their grain, and in the morning the Lord caused a deep sleep to come upon the Lamanites. This was an even more miraculous escape than the people of Limhi's escape. After a couple of days, Alma and his people stopped to camp in a valley and rejoice in their freedom, lifting up their voices in praise of their God. And the voice of the Lord said unto Alma, "Haste thee and get thou and this people out of this land, for the Lamanites have awakened and do pursue thee; therefore get thee out of this land, and I will stop the Lamanites in this valley that they come no further in pursuit of this people."[83]

I share this story of Limhi, Zeniff, and Alma the Elder because some of you reading this may have already made some mistakes that make you feel that you cannot be forgiven. This is false. Zeniff made mistakes, and his life ended in great peace and goodness. Alma made mistakes, and so did all the people of the land of Zeniff.

We learn from this story that sometimes it takes time to fully escape the consequences of our mistakes. Forgiveness and consequences are different things. We can be forgiven of our sins while still suffering the consequences of them. Consequences are natural, and

82. Mosiah 24:15.
83. Mosiah 24:23.

forgiveness does not make all of them suddenly and magically go away. Limhi's people suffered for not choosing to hearken to Abinadi or to Alma. Their enslavement to the Lamanites was unfair, but it was a natural consequence of losing the protection of the Lord through disobedience, and a natural consequence of not following the prophetic words of Abinadi or Alma.

Alma found himself suddenly face-to-face with his former sins when he and his people were placed in bondage to Amulon. He had been forgiven years before, but Amulon would not recognize that forgiveness nor the source of all forgiveness. In a way, both the Limhites and the people of Alma had to endure what seemed like an unfair consequence of their sins. They were in bondage even after repenting. The people of Limhi fought against their bondage three times and suffered great losses each time. Once they humbled themselves, their rescue came. The people of Alma took a different route: they didn't fight against their consequences, but instead *submitted cheerfully.* As a result of their humility and faith, the Lord rescued the people of Alma in a truly miraculous way.

In both instances, the people were pursued as they tried to escape. With the people of Limhi, after following for a couple of days, the Lamanites were no longer able to follow their tracks. I see this as symbolic of the Lord's forgiveness. So complete was the Lord's forgiveness that, after a time, he removed all stain of the people's sins, so that their sins truly followed them no more. Their consequences were removed. Eventually.

In the example from the people of Alma, the Lord's intervention is even more dramatic. Amulon sent an army after Alma, but the Lord flat out stopped them in their tracks. Because Alma and his people submitted cheerfully to the long-term consequences of their errors, even though they knew they had been forgiven long before,

the Lord eventually stopped others from continuing to hold those sins against them.

It doesn't take an Amulon to hold your past choices against you. Sometimes it can take time for even good people to change their perceptions of your goodness. Fighting against these perceptions often only serves to confirm their suspicions. Submitting cheerfully to these individual ironies is often the best course of action.

My young brothers and sisters, just like Amulon and the Lamanites, Satan will pursue you as you seek to repent, but I promise that you can always stay one step ahead. Forgiveness is available to you through the Atonement of Jesus Christ; however, forgiveness does not erase the immediate or even long-term natural consequences of bad decisions. If you find yourself in the midst of those consequences, surrounded by some who cannot yet see the mighty change of heart you have experienced, or who do not yet trust you, please learn from Alma and his people. Do not fight against natural consequences to bad decisions like the people of Limhi fought against the Lamanites. Earning back trust from parents, siblings, friends, and others you may have hurt takes time and cannot be demanded. If you submit cheerfully to the Lord's efforts to chasten you, like the people of Alma, I promise you that one day your sins will no longer follow you. The tracks left behind by your past will disappear and the Lord will stop your pursuers. You will truly be free!

Now, my time is almost over, but I want you to do something for me. Go get an old, worn-out T-shirt and a pair of scissors. I'll wait . . .

Ready? Good. Remember the title of liberty? Remember how Moroni went out to the public square and waved it around? He didn't know how people would respond, but soon people ran to him in droves. Like he said earlier, I was the first one to arrive. After hearing his words, I ran home, grabbed my sword and armor, and took an article of clothing back with me. I tore it and threw it

at Moroni's feet as a covenant and promise to support the title of liberty.

If you feel comfortable doing so, I'd like you to take your old shirt and use the scissors to cut off the bottom four inches, all the way around. That should give you a ring of material. Then cut the ring in the middle somewhere so you have one long, four-inch-wide strip of material instead of a circle. Stretch it out, and then take a thick permanent pen and write the full title of liberty on one side: "In memory of our God, our religion, and freedom, and our peace, our wives, and our children."[84]

84. Alma 46:12.

Then, on the other side of the fabric, write down some of the bullet points from the captain's logs found at the end of each chapter. You can write them all down, or just the ones you believe will help you the most, whatever you like. Write what will help you on the path to righteousness.

After you have finished, you may see that this doesn't look much like a flag. That's on purpose. I'm not asking you to fly it above your house. I'm asking you to hang it on your doorknob, your chair, a hook, or something else in your room. This torn or cut piece of fabric is a symbol of the promise you and I and others made to follow the title of liberty.

If you ever feel tempted to give in to boredom, anger, tiredness, or just curiosity and do something you should not do, I want you to pick up your personal title of liberty and wrap it around your eyes and head like a blindfold. Then remove it and take a moment to reread what you've written on the fabric. This is how we raise the title of liberty today. We don't live in blind faith, but we do close our eyes to pride, to selfishness, and to deceit. We close our eyes to temptation and sin. We pay them no heed. Just like Amalickiah, sin and temptation seek to bring you into bondage. Do not give in to them. I believe in you, my friends, and I know that if you build your plan around Christ, you cannot fail.

CHAPTER 19

GOODBYE FOR NOW

Godspeed, my friend!
Don't forget to ask for one last glass of chocolate milk before you close the book!
Have I told you how much better chocolate milk is when made with whole milk?
Don't even get me started on half and half!

CHAPTER 20

EPILOGUE

Hey, guys, Moronihah here! My dad asked me to drop by real quick with a little reminder. A few years after my father passed away and I became the chief captain, we had a very interesting experience. After the Amalickiah war, we experienced approximately fifteen years of peace. Then a large and mighty man was made captain of the Lamanite army and led a numberless host in war against us. His name was Coriantumr.

Our cities were fortified and we felt very strong and safe, having followed the protocols my father had established. Nevertheless, Coriantumr caught us off guard. Instead of attacking the border cities, he marched straight into Zarahemla, killed our chief judge, and took over the city. We were shocked and surprised by his boldness.

My father wants me to remind you that even after you overcome whatever it is that is tempting you, every now and again Satan will suddenly and boldly attack you when and where you least expect it. You have to be ready for these sudden onslaughts and recognize them for what they are. Do not walk away from the successes you have achieved and the goodness you have attained. Do not let Satan convince you that you have never changed just because you felt unexpectedly tempted. Satan is like a caged wild animal who tests the fences to see if the electricity is still on. He will do so suddenly, violently, and without warning, no matter how strong your fences have been or how long you have been safe.

Continuing in prayer and scripture study will keep the electricity on, but the key is to pay those temptations no heed.[85]

We quickly disposed of Coriantumr, because by plunging right into the middle of our country, he left himself surrounded by powerful defenses developed over years of preparation. He was a sitting duck, just like Satan will be for you when he throws himself at your fences like a tantrum-throwing toddler. Our forces attacked Coriantumr from all sides, killed him, and expelled his army. Nevertheless, Coriantumr caused damage and a few days of great fear. Do not let any Coriantumrs into your midst, and be sure to recognize them for who they are and dispose of them quickly.

Alright, that's all I've got! You have a good one—and by the way, what do you think of my man bun? Pretty nice, eh?

THE END

85. 1 Nephi 8:33.

ABOUT THE AUTHOR

Sean Nobmann was born in Petaluma, California, and raised on Mercer Island, Washington. He served a mission for The Church of Jesus Christ of Latter-day Saints in Santiago, Chile. Sean and his wife, Katherine Robbins Nobmann, met as MTC teachers before graduating from BYU. Sean enjoys coaching his four sons' sports teams, especially flag football. His sons are sure he didn't write this book because, "Dad, unlike you, the book is actually funny." After graduating from Duke Law, Sean worked at a large international law firm in Houston. He and his family now live in Utah, where he runs his own law firm. On his website, www.seannobmann.com, you can read his blog and learn more about his background and experience.

ABOUT THE ILLUSTRATOR

Norman Shurtliff grew up in Northern British Columbia, Canada. He spent much of his time at the family greenhouses, where he and his siblings explored the endless outdoors, built forts, told stories, and invented games. Norman's imagination grew with him, and so did his love of comics and game design. He served a mission for The Church of Jesus Christ of Latter-day Saints in Auckland, New Zealand. He received a BS of horticulture at BYU–Idaho and later, with the encouragement of his wife, received a BS of media arts and animation at the Art Institute of Salt Lake City. Norman now lives in Twin Falls, Idaho, with his wife and their three adventurous children. He is the author of *Amazing Scriptures*, which combines his childhood love of mazes and comics with his love of the Book of Mormon stories.

SCAN TO VISIT

www.seannobmann.com

www.normanshurtliff.com